AN UNDERGROUND WORLD
THE CATACOMBS OF PARIS

Sylvie Robin
Jean-Pierre Gély
Marc Viré

PARIS MUSÉES
LES MUSÉES DE LA VILLE DE PARIS
| LES COLLECTIONS DE LA VILLE DE PARIS

Introduction to a subterranean world

Descending from place Denfert-Rochereau, 62 metres above sea level, to the Catacombs, 20 metres below, is to travel back in time some forty-five million years, traversing a succession of rock strata until reaching the layers of limestone corresponding to the 'Lutetian' geological level of the Tertiary (Cenozoic Era), a geological time-span of some forty-eight to forty million years. This period, precisely identified in the Catacombs, is named after Paris's Latin name, *Lutetia*.

It was this beautiful light beige limestone, so highly prized by Parisian quarrymen from the most ancient times to the early 20th century, that provided much of Paris's construction stone. The medieval underground quarries beneath the Denfert-Rochereau neighbourhood, abandoned now for several centuries, were reinforced to receive bones from cemeteries that fell into disuse before the Revolution. Bones continued to be transferred there until the 1960s, and for two centuries now, an increasing number of visitors have discovered this subterranean world.

Paris's municipal ossuary, known as 'the Catacombs', reveals a fraction of the Earth's geological evolution and the history of those who built Paris and whose bones were consigned to oblivion there, a story that unfolds for visitors as they venture into the galleries of the Catacombs.

fig. 1
Geologic description,
noting the age
of the rocks.

FROM PLACE DENFERT-ROCHEREAU TO THE CATACOMBS

Concealed by the masonry of the steps leading down to the Catacombs, beneath road fill and shallow archaeological layers, on descent the geological strata become increasingly ancient. This is characteristic of the superimposed layers in a sedimentary basin, such as the Parisian Basin, whose centre is occupied by Paris.

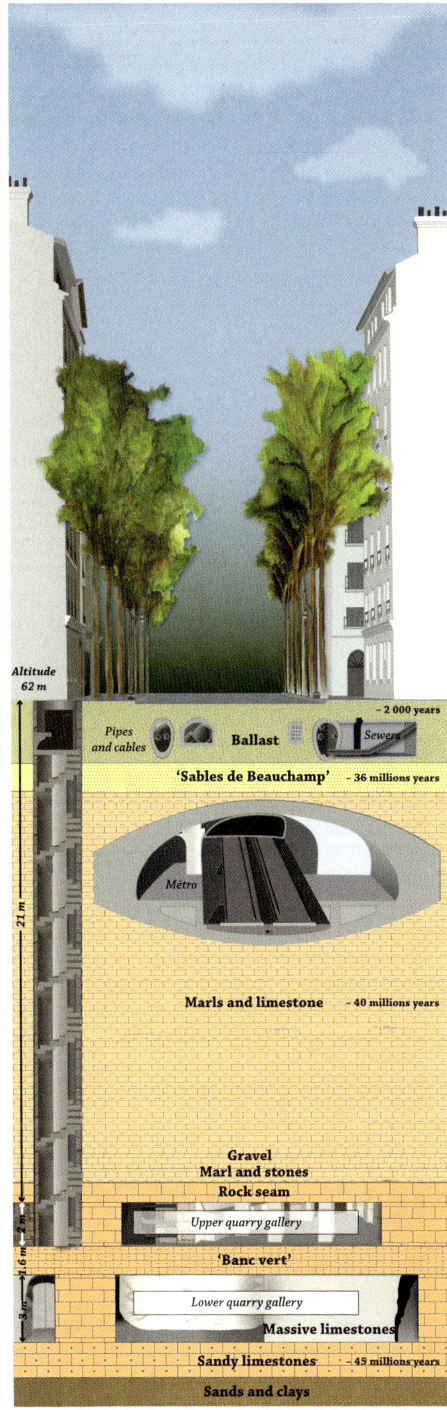

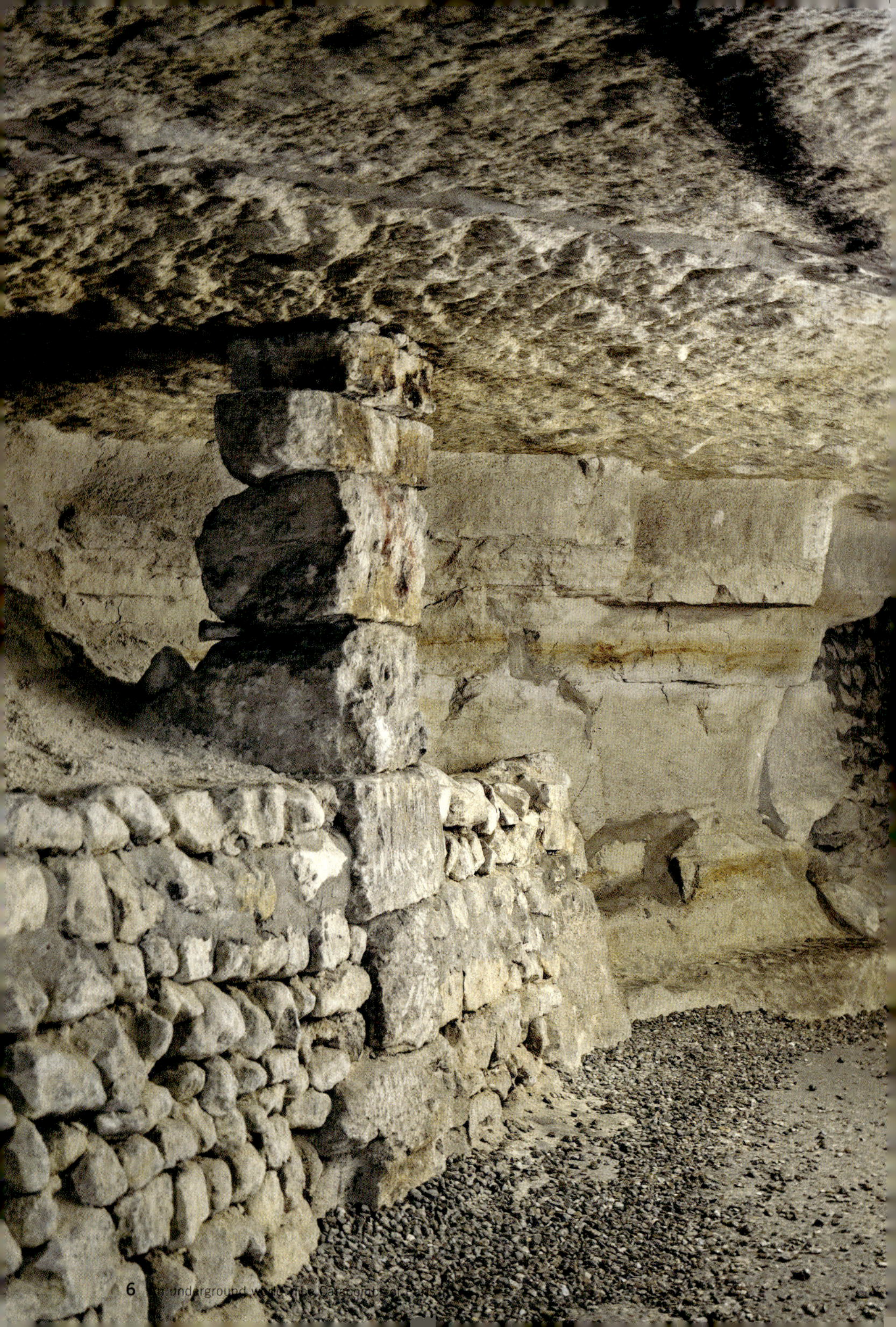

fig. 2
Workshop area

FROM THE SEA TO QUARRIES

Stratigraphic cross-section

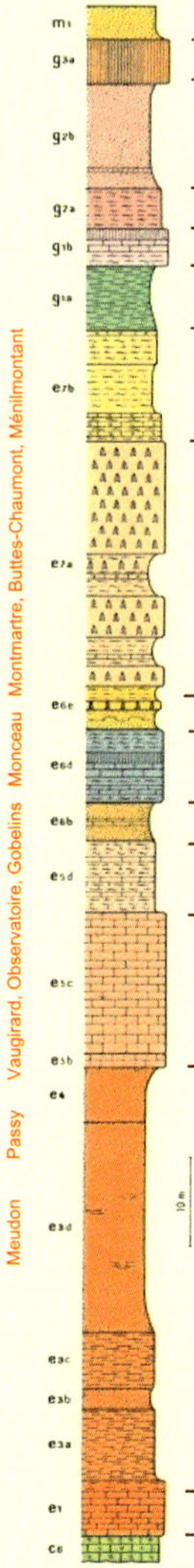

Formation (age)	Using
Lozère sands (Pliocene)	Mortar
'Montmorency Millstone' (Upper Rupelian [Stampian])	Building stone, dimension stone, ballasting, millstones
Fontainebleau sands and sandstones (Upper Rupelian [Stampian])	Mortar, building stone, dimension stone, paving stone, glass
'Oyster' clays (Lower Rupelian [Stampian])	Roofing tiles and bricks
Brie and Sannois limestones (Lower Rupelian [Sannoisian])	Building stone, ballasting, lime
Green limestones (Lower Rupelian [Sannoisian])	Roofing tiles and bricks
Supra-gypsic clays (Upper Priabonian [Ludian])	Roofing tiles and bricks
1st gypsum mass (Middle Priabonian [Ludian])	Building stone, plaster
'Spearhead' clays (Middle Priabonian [Ludian])	Roofing tiles and bricks
2nd gypsum mass (Middle Priabonian [Ludian])	
Cerith snail clays (Middle Priabonian [Ludian])	Building stone, plaster
3rd gypsum mass (Middle Priabonian [Ludian])	Plaster
Pholadomi clay (Lower Priabonian [Ludian])	
Monceau sands and 4th mass of gypsum (Upper Bartonian [Lower Marinesian])	Mortar
Saint-Ouen and Ducy limestones (Lower Bartonian [Auversian])	Building stone, paving stones, ballasting, lime
'Sables de Beauchamp' (Lower Bartonian [Auversian])	Mortar, glass
Marl and stones (Upper Lutetian)	Building stone, ballasting, lime
Coarse limestone (Lower to upper Lutetian)	Mortar, building stone, dimension stone, lime
Upper sands (Middle Ypresian [Cuisian])	Mortar
Cuise sands (Middle Ypresian [Cuisian])	Mortar
False clays (Lower Ypresian [Sparnacian])	Roofing tiles and bricks, lignites
Auteuil sands (Lower Ypresian [Sparnacian])	Mortar
Malleable clay (Lower Ypresian [Sparnacian])	Roofing tiles and bricks, lignites
Meudon limestone and clays (Danian)	Building stone
White chalk (Upper Campanian)	Building stone, lime, coat

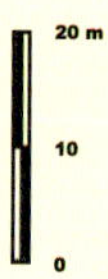

Genesis of the Parisian Basin

Paris occupies the centre of a large sedimentary basin, the Parisian Basin. It is bordered by the Ardennes to the north, the Vosges to the east, the Massif Central to the south and the Armorican Massif to the west, the ancient base of western Europe following the formation of a supercontinent, Pangaea, 350 million years ago. The erosion of the mountains and the dislocation of this supercontinent enabled the sea to deposit more than some 3,000 metres of sediment over a 300 million-year period on the site of the future Parisian Basin.

fig. 3
Stratigraphic cross-section. The geology of Paris offered the mineral resources which historically favoured the city's growth.

A USE FOR EACH MATERIAL

Since Antiquity, the great variety of sedimentary layers in evidence from the banks of the Seine and the Bièvre to the heights of Montmartre and Belleville have provided Parisians with abundant construction materials: sand for mixing mortar; sandstone for paving stones; clay for bricks, tiles and roofing tiles; limestone for building stone, dimension stone and lime production; and gypsum for plaster.
The only materials the city lacked were slate, brought from Anjou and the Ardennes, and iron, lead, bronze and tin, which were imported from further afield in France and from neighbouring countries.

This area slowly began to take on the physiognomy it has had for the last 65 million years, since the time when the dinosaurs disappeared.

From then on the sea only occupied the centre of the basin for intermittent periods. For the last 25 million years, the sea has made only brief incursions as far as Anjou. The basin, distant foreland of the Pyrenees and the Alps, was warped by the upthrust of the Massif Central and the Ardennes. The rising of the edge of the Rhine rift valley created the Vosges and the successive cuestas of Lorraine and Champagne. The expansion of the Atlantic created the attenuated reliefs of Brittany and Cotentin. For the last two million years, the basin's overall uprising has obliged watercourses to deepen their beds, sometimes cutting into successive sedimentary layers. The broad meanders of the Seine, and its tributary the Bièvre, have modelled Paris's present-day relief to a height of about one hundred metres. This configuration gave the valley's inhabitants access to an extraordinary variety of rocks and therefore the materials required to build a city. But only one geological strata could provide high-quality building stone, the Lutetian limestone extracted mainly on the Left Bank of the Seine.

The Catacombs: cradle of modern geology

Most of the layers of Lutetian limestone are visible in the Catacombs, principally in the reservoir called the 'quarry-mens' footbath'. In 1815 Louis-Étienne François Héricart de Thury, general inspector of underground works for the administrative division, the Seine department, was the first to precisely describe the successive geological lay-

fig. 4
Historical cross-section described by Héricart de Thury, with the quarrymen's vernacular name for each layer of rock.

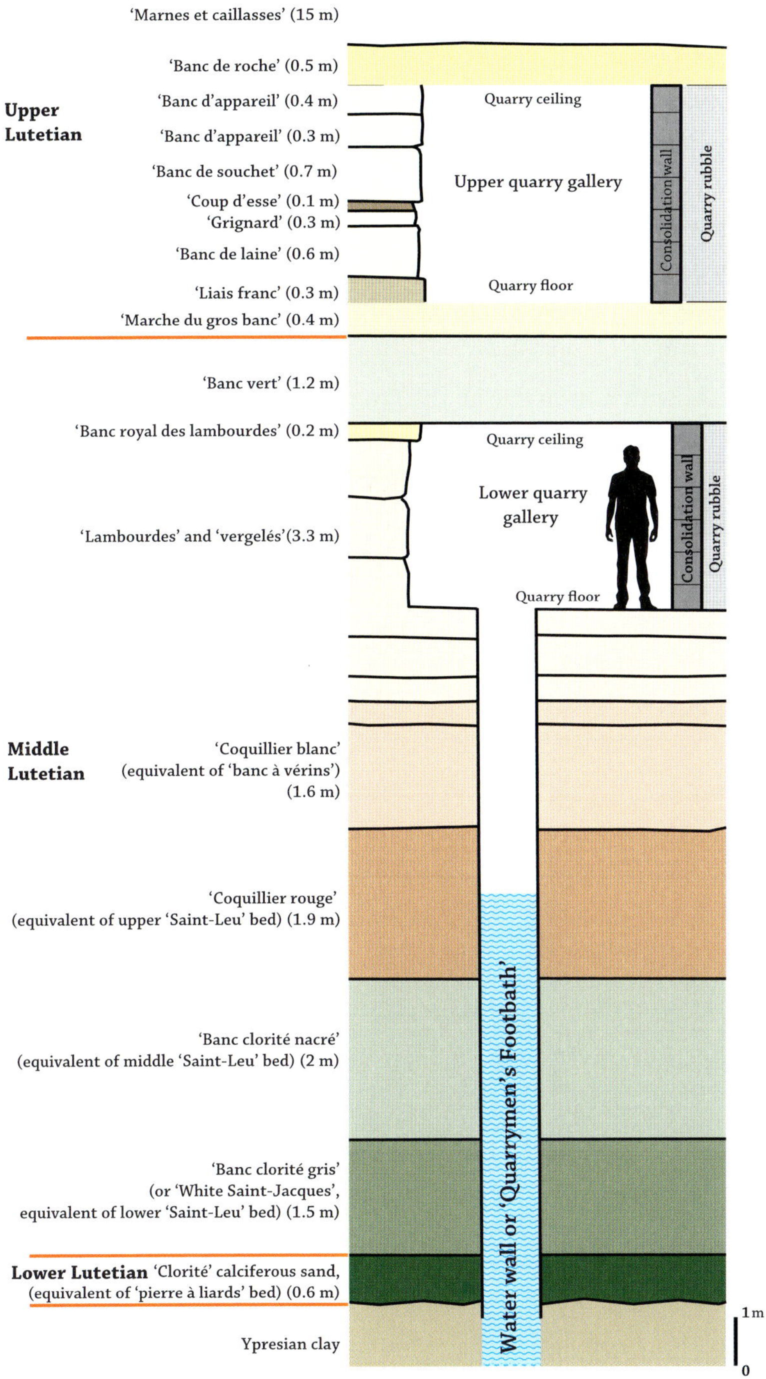
'Marnes et caillasses' (15 m)
'Banc de roche' (0.5 m)
Upper Lutetian
'Banc d'appareil' (0.4 m)
'Banc d'appareil' (0.3 m)
'Banc de souchet' (0.7 m)
'Coup d'esse' (0.1 m)
'Grignard' (0.3 m)
'Banc de laine' (0.6 m)
'Liais franc' (0.3 m)
'Marche du gros banc' (0.4 m)
Quarry ceiling
Upper quarry gallery
Quarry floor
Consolidation wall
Quarry rubble
'Banc vert' (1.2 m)
'Banc royal des lambourdes' (0.2 m)
'Lambourdes' and 'vergelés'(3.3 m)
Quarry ceiling
Lower quarry gallery
Quarry floor
Consolidation wall
Quarry rubble
Middle Lutetian
'Coquillier blanc' (equivalent of 'banc à vérins') (1.6 m)
'Coquillier rouge' (equivalent of upper 'Saint-Leu' bed) (1.9 m)
'Banc clorité nacré' (equivalent of middle 'Saint-Leu' bed) (2 m)
'Banc clorité gris' (or 'White Saint-Jacques', equivalent of lower 'Saint-Leu' bed) (1.5 m)
Lower Lutetian
'Clorité' calciferous sand, (equivalent of 'pierre à liards' bed) (0.6 m)
Ypresian clay
Water wall or 'Quarrymen's Footbath'
1m
0

ers visible there. In 1883, Albert-Auguste de Lapparent (1839–1908) established this geological cross-section as the international definition of a period in the Earth's history: the Lutetian layer. The Lutetian limestone in the Versailles and Reims regions contains an extraordinary variety of marine fauna in an excellent state of conservation. Naturalists had begun classify this fossilised fauna in the late 18th century. From 1802 to 1809, Jean-Baptiste de Monet, Chevalier de Lamarck (1744–1829), published his monumental *Mémoires sur les fossiles des environs de Paris*, the first classification of the fossilised marine invertebrates of the Tertiary Period, accompanied by notions of the evolution of the species and the geographic and climatic changes during the Earth's history. But precisely why was there such marine diversity at that time?

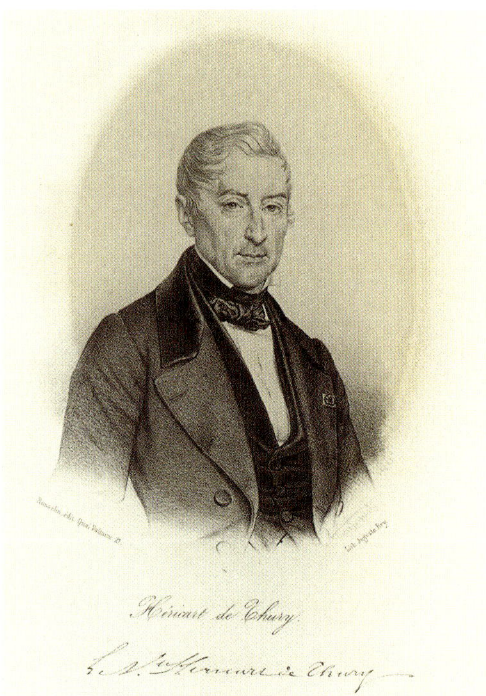

fig. 5
Viscount Louis-Étienne François Héricart de Thury (1776–1854) published *Description of the Catacombs of Paris* in 1815. Lithograph by Auguste Bry after a drawing by Toussaint, published by Rosselin. and, following the reorganisation of the ossuary in 1809, opened the Catacombs to the public.

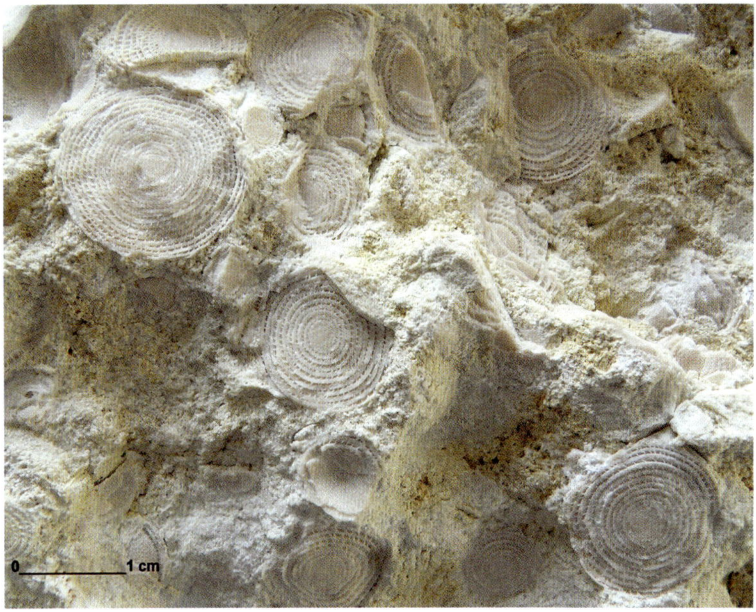

fig. 6
Limestone containing *Nummulites laevigatus*, commonly known as 'liard stone' after a small medieval French coin.

Formation of the Lutetian limestone

At the beginning of the Lutetian period, the North Sea progressively invaded Belgium then northern France, reaching present-day Paris at the end of the lower Lutetian period. The shoreline was bordered by broad, sandy beaches, while out to sea, unicellular creatures, nummulites, accumulated at a depth of some fifty metres. In Paris, there are a few marine debris, transported by sea currents and the waves, in the first sandy levels of the Lutetian layer. A rich tropical marine fauna lived in this open sea. Large bivalves and gastropods inhabited the seabed, and sharks, turtles and a variety of fish shoaled in the currents that swept the Parisian gulf. The variety of marine habitats increased as the gulf extended southwards.

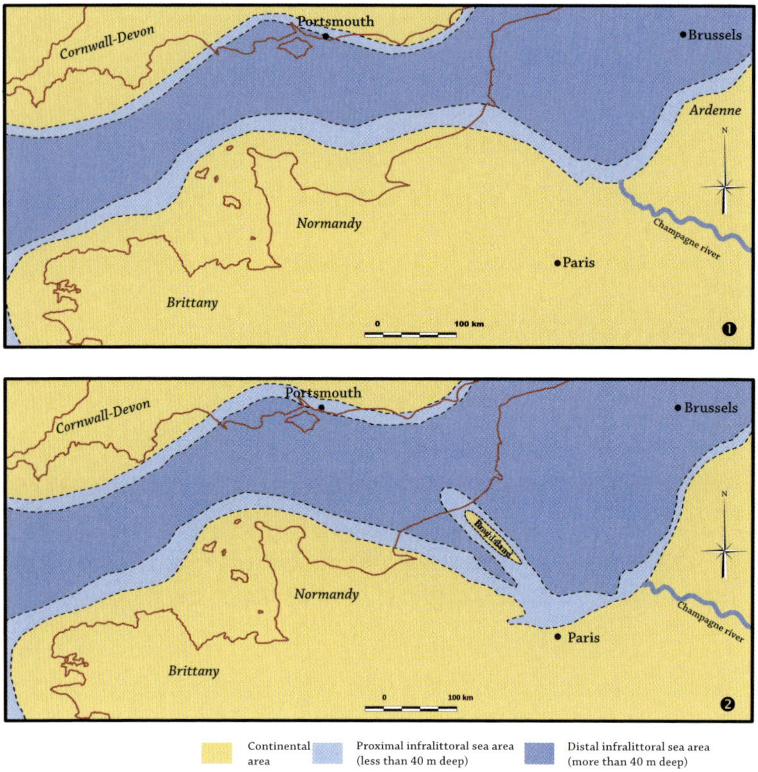

fig. 7
Paleogeographic maps of the lower Lutetian. The Lutetian stage spans some eight million years and consists of three periods: the lower, middle and upper Lutetian. At the beginning of the lower Lutetian (1), the sea had not yet reached Paris. At the end of the lower Lutetian (2), during the deposit of limestone containing *Nummulites laevigatus*, the shoreline was located where Paris is today.

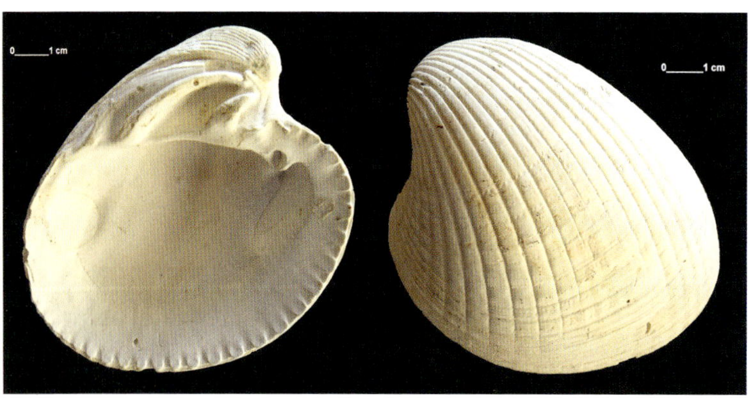

fig. 8
Venericor planicosta, a large bivalve abundant during the lower Lutetian.

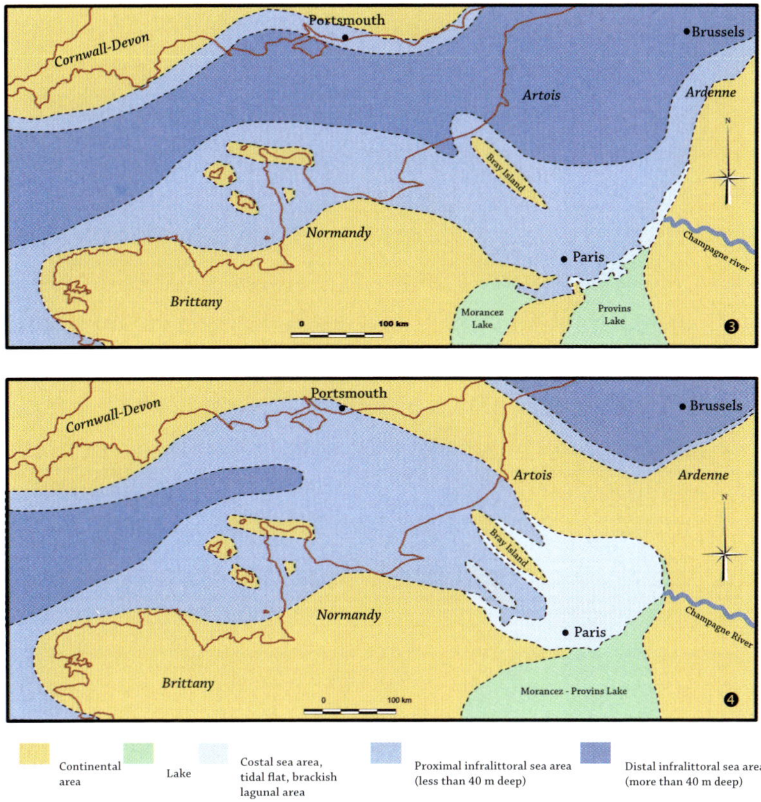

fig. 9
Paleogeographic maps of the middle and upper Lutetian. In the middle Lutetian (3), the sea reached its maximum extension southward. In the upper Lutetian (4), the sea, cut off to the north by the Artois Dome, gradually withdrew from the middle of the Parisian Basin.

The Lutetian sea: one of the most biodiverse environments in the Earth's history

In the middle Lutetian period, as the sea was continuing to advance south of Paris to form a vast gulf opening on to the North Sea and the nearby Atlantic, its depth decreased as it was gradually filled by sands and calciferous muds. The sea was home to the largest known gastropod, *Campanile giganteum*, which could grow to a length of 70 centimetres. The marine biodiversity around the edges of this gulf, one of the richest in the Earth's history, is recorded by numerous fossil imprints in the limestone, the shells having dissolved.

At the beginning of the upper Lutetian period, the Pyrenees were created by the collision between the Iberian and Eurasian tectonic plates. One of the distant echoes of this event, the uplifting of the Artois Dome, separated the North Sea from the Parisian gulf, which remained connected to the Atlantic via broad channels separated by islands. The gulf gradually became a huge bay fringed with mangroves and coastal lagoons. Its undiversified fauna could adapt to great variations in salinity and seawater temperature. Its aquatic plants teemed with miliolidae, the minute foraminifera which became the main components of limestone, and cerith snails lived at a depth of a few metres. The

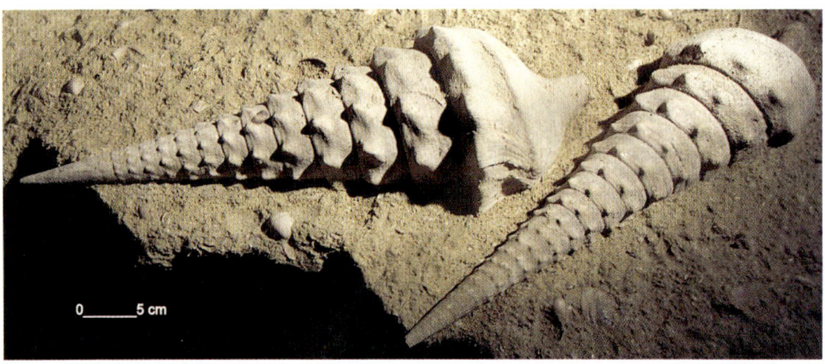

fig. 10
Shells of the large gastropod *Campanile giganteum*, perfectly preserved in soft limestone near Reims. In Paris, this species is sometimes present in white fossil limestone.

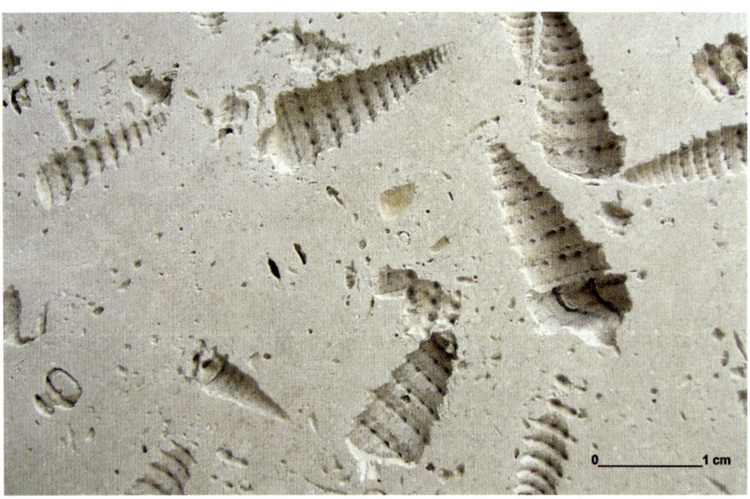

fig. 11
Limestone containing miliolidae and moulds of cerith snails. In the upper Lutetian limestone layers, very often only one species of cerith proliferated. These fossils can sometimes be seen in the roofs of galleries and in the supporting pillars left by quarrymen. They are also visible in the walls of medieval monuments in Paris.

sea gradually withdrew from the gulf, leaving an immense lagoon where gypsum crystallised as seawater evaporated (depositing marl and loose stones).

From one world to another

After the Lutetian, the calciferous marine muds solidified into limestone of varying hardness buried beneath more recent sedimentary layers. Under the tectonic constraints of the Pyrenees then the Alps, these layers fractured and bent to form the Medon anticline. As the Seine has gradually eroded the rocks in its path over the last two million years, it has exposed the Lutetian limestone in its valley walls. For two thousand years this limestone has been intensively exploited as Paris's prime construction material, mainly on the Left Bank of the Seine (5th, 6th, 13th, 14th and 15th arrondissements), to a lesser extent on the Right Bank (12th and 16th arrondissements), and on a massive scale in the capital's southern suburbs.

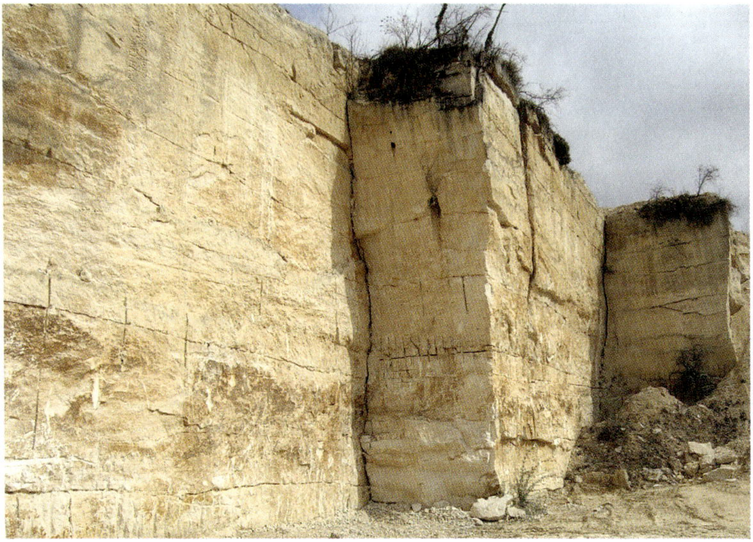

fig. 12
Major tectonic fractures (joints) in Lutetian limestone in a quarry in the Oise valley.

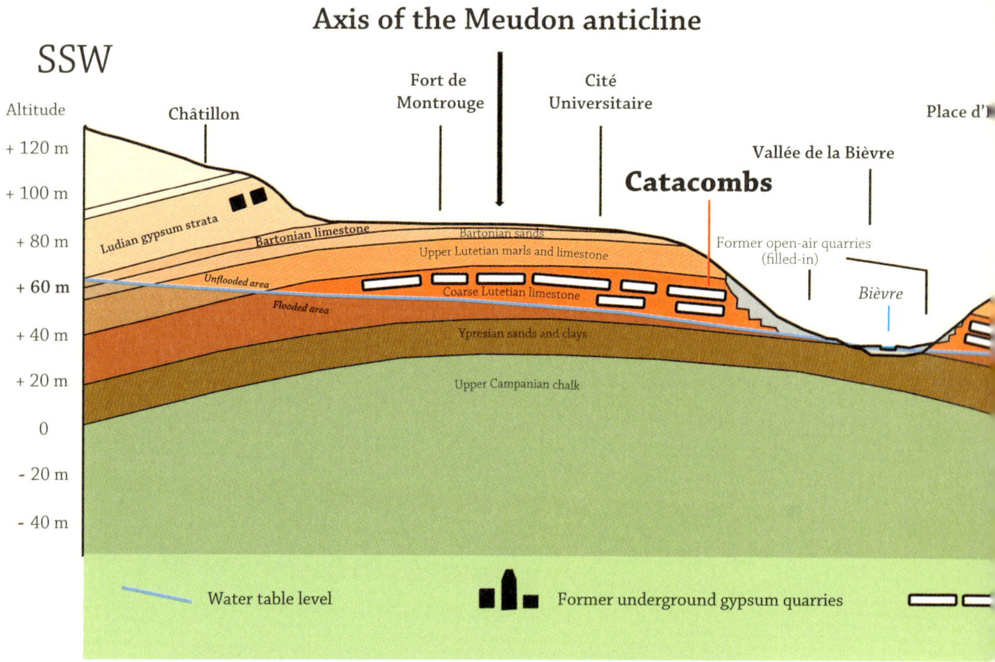

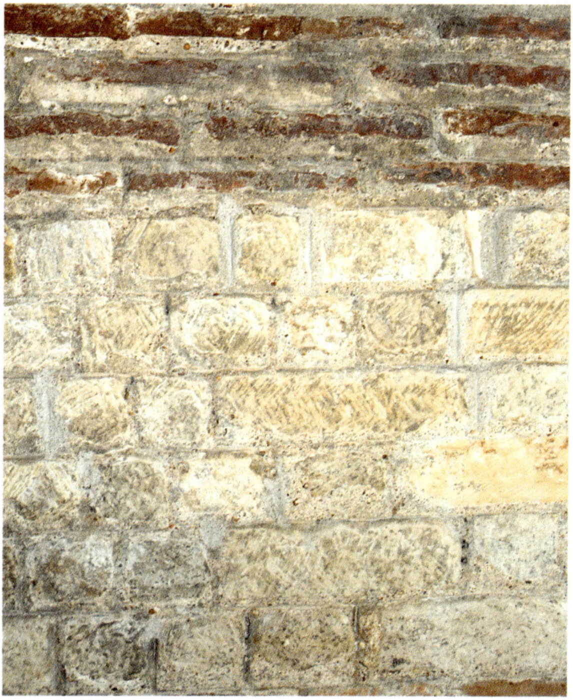

fig. 14
Small apparatus alternating bricks and *opus mixtum* (Roman construction technique) in the frigidarium of the Thermes de Cluny.

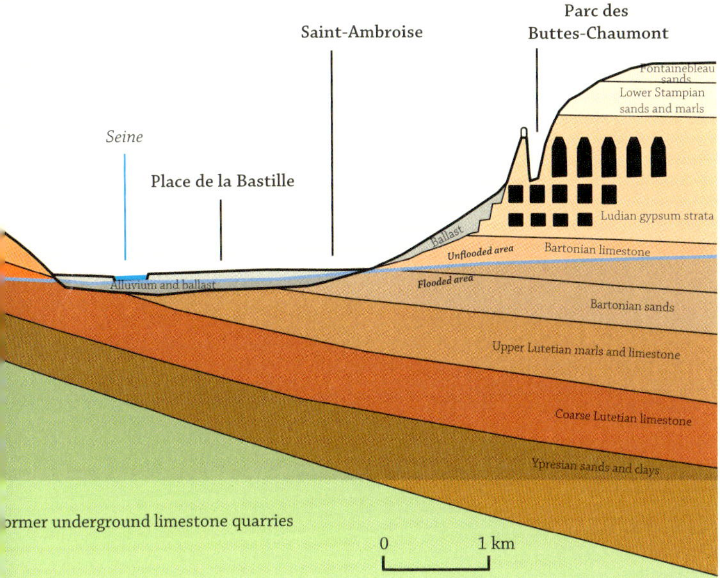

fig. 13
Geological cross-section of Paris between the Buttes-Chaumont to the north and Châtillon in the south, showing the importance of the Meudon anticline in Parisian geology and the history of the region's stone quarries.

History of Paris's quarries from Antiquity to the Middle Ages

fig. 15
Schema of an open-air quarry: the unused upper levels have been removed to expose the stone to be extracted.

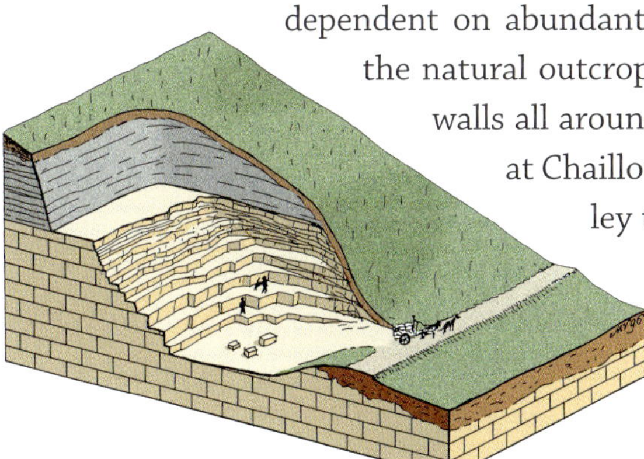

In Antiquity, Lutetian limestone was extracted in open-air quarries that did not require complex technology but was dependent on abundant manpower. Quarrying began in the natural outcrops of Lutetian limestone in valley walls all around Paris, at Charenton to the east, at Chaillot to the west and in the Bièvre valley to the south. The small cut stones in the Arènes de Lutèce and the Thermes de Cluny are typical of the quarries in the Jardin des Plantes and Saint-Médard areas (5th arrondissement).

As the quarry face advanced into the hillside, the quality of the stone exposed increased, and fine dimension stone could be increasingly used for Lutetia's monuments.

The Merovingians quarried little stone, preferring to carve their sarcophagi from stone salvaged from the ancient city's edifices. Most of their stone was imported from the Oise valley and Burgundy. The few blocks still extracted locally helped to maintain Parisian quarrying skills.

Around the year 1000, several major church construction projects marked the gradual resumption of building in stone. Little stone could now be salvaged from the ancient city, and stone again began to be extracted from local quarries.

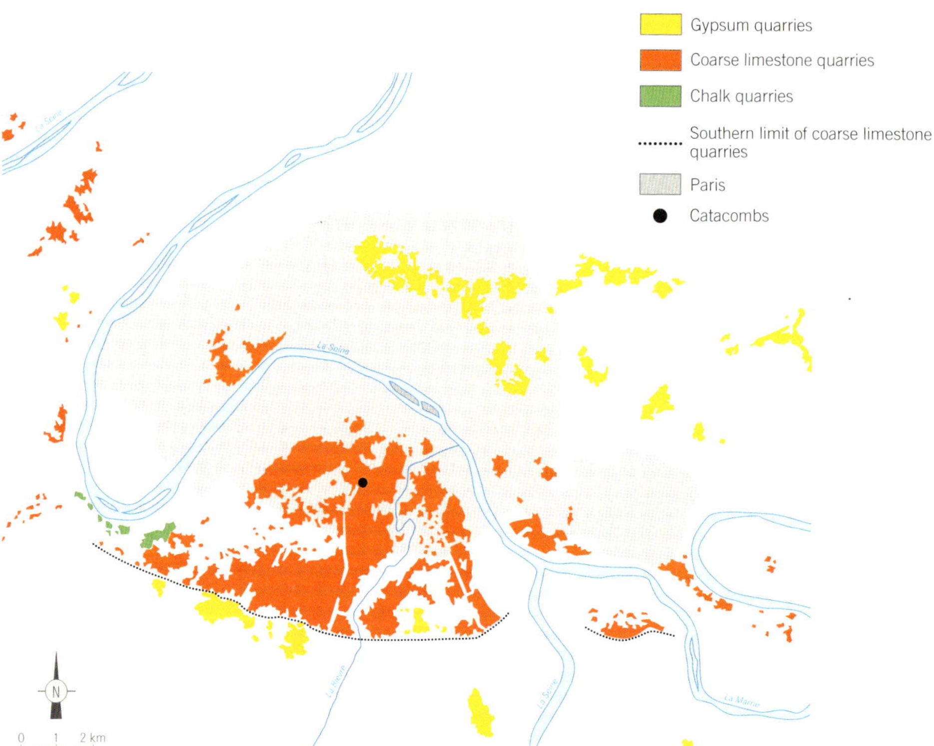

fig. 16
Map of the surface and underground quarries in Paris and its suburbs. Beyond the quarries' southern limit along the Meudon anticline's southern slope, the Lutetian limestone gradually descends beneath the water table, rendering its exploitation impossible

From open-air to underground quarrying

Stone quarrying developed again during the course of the 12th century. A succession of major constructions demanded ever more stone: Saint-Martin-des-Champs (1150), Saint-Germain-des-Prés (1155), the gargantuan project of Notre-Dame cathedral (1160), the Louvre fortress (1180) and the six-kilometre-long city walls. New quarries were opened, often extensions of ancient filled-in quarries. The Bièvre valley in Paris became a major production site.

When open-air quarries became too deep, they went underground. Quarrymen hollowed out 'bouches de cavage' (tunnelling mouths) in the rock face, advancing along galleries to reach stone deeper in the rock. In these quarries, masses of stone called 'turned pillars' were left in place to support the terrain above.

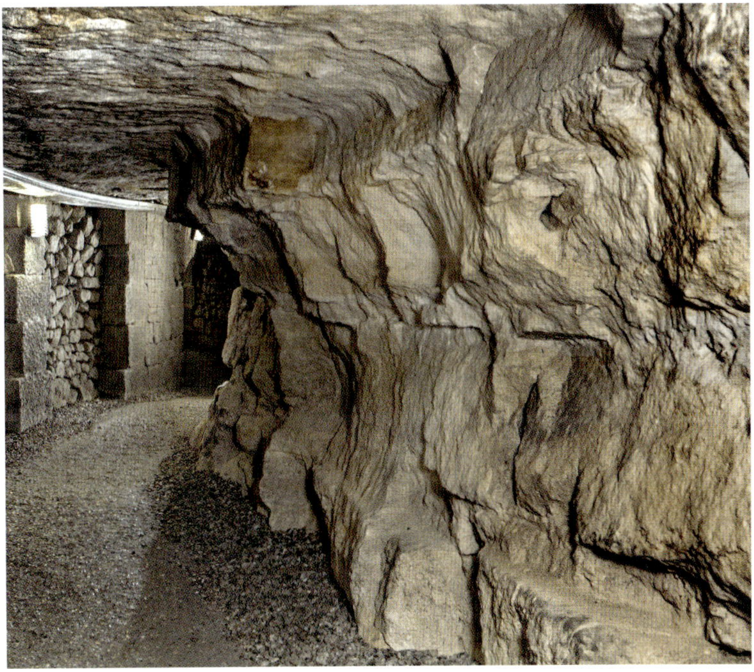

fig. 17
'Turned pillar' in the medieval quarry at the entrance to the ossuary.

A new, subterranean world was created as quarrymen ventured further and further into the limestone beneath the plateau. In the 14th century stone began to be raised to the surface using manpowered wheels, via shafts descending into the quarry.

In the late Middle Ages quarrymen developed the 'hagues et bourrages' method, consisting of extracting all the rock in a gallery without leaving pillars. To support the quarry roof, quarrymen now filled in all the voids with extraction and cutting waste ('bourrages'), which were then consolidated by stone walls ('hagues') and pillars composed of large blocks, leaving access routes between the extraction spaces and the shafts.

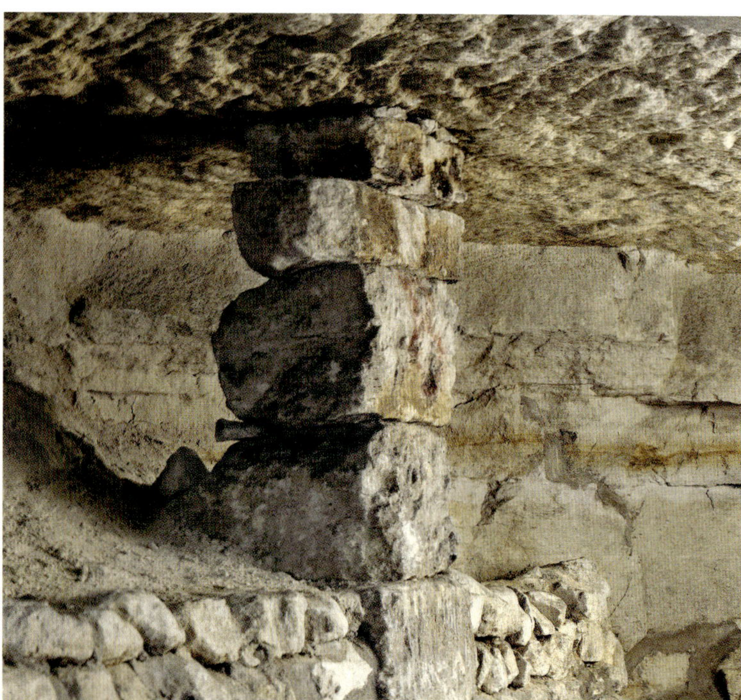

fig. 18
Manmade pillars and consolidations in the Catacombs.

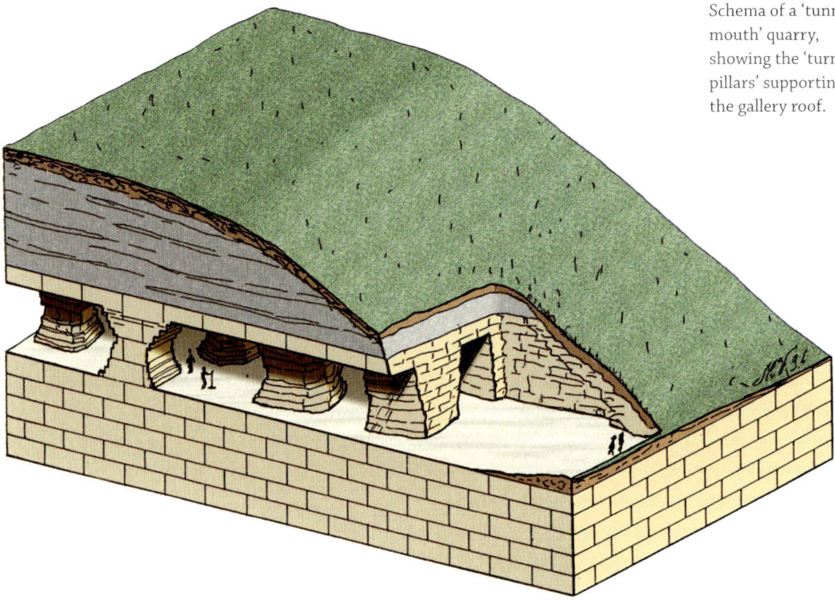

fig. 19
Schema of a 'tunnel mouth' quarry, showing the 'turned pillars' supporting the gallery roof.

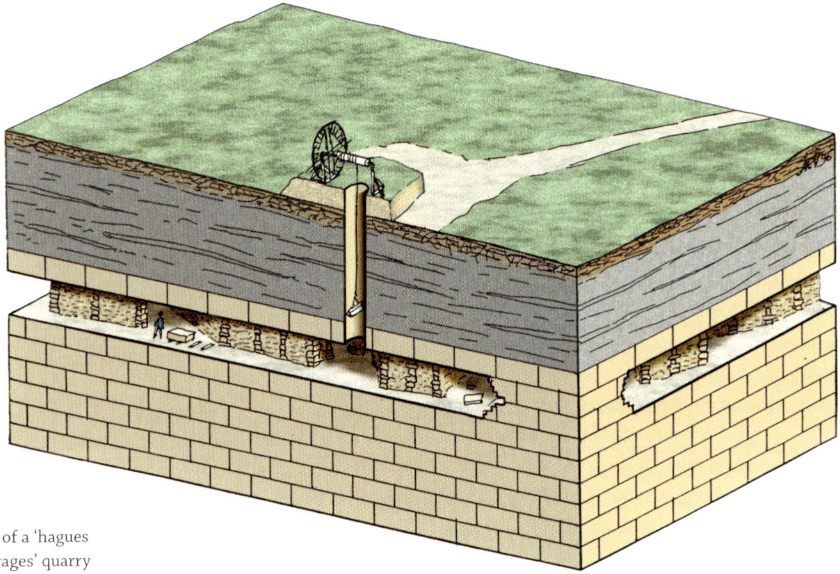

fig. 20
Schema of a 'hagues et bourrages' quarry with extraction by wheel and shaft.

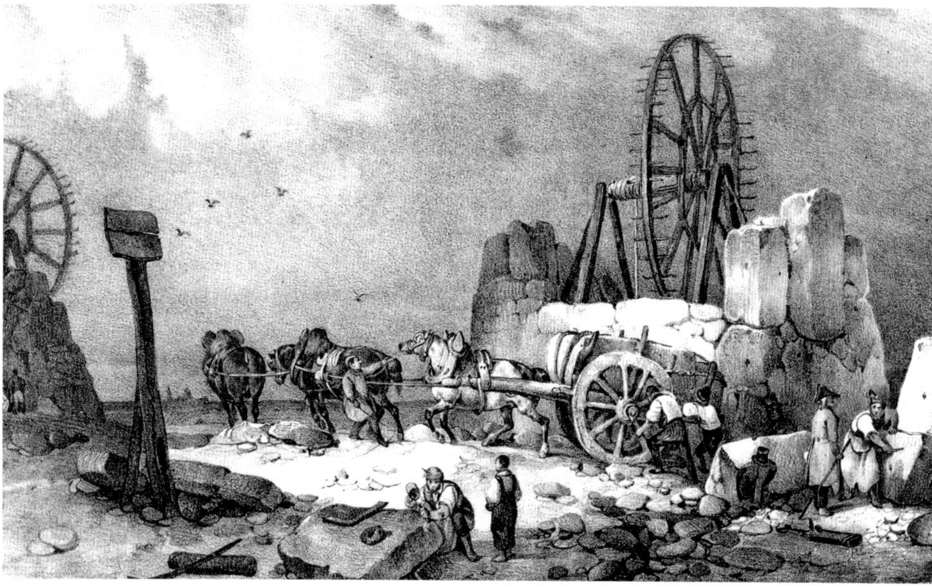

The Tombe-Issoire quarries

fig. 21
Quarryman's cart. Lithograph by Charles-Étienne-Pierre Motte (1785–1836), after a drawing by Victor Jean Adam (1801–1866), between 1828 and 1830, Musée Carnavalet, Paris.

The *cardo maximus* (main street) of Lutetia corresponds to the present-day Rue Saint-Jacques. Outside the city's southern limit, this road continued along Rue du Faubourg-Saint-Jacques and Rue de la Tombe-Issoire on its way to Orléans. In the Middle Ages, underground quarries developed along this road, near the Notre-Dame-des-Champs priory (now the Lycée Lavoisier, 5th arrondissement), on the site of the Val-de-Grâce and in the southern 5th arrondissement, and between Rue Claude-Bernard and Boulevard Arago, then an area of fields and vines. In the late Middle Ages extraction extended towards the south of the large 'Tombe-Issoire' or 'Port-Mahon' quarry, site of the future ossuary.

The Tombe-Issoire site belonged to the Order of the Knights Hospitaller, and more precisely to the commandery bearing the name of Saint-Jean-de-Latran from the end of the 16th century. Around 1130, the order established a commandry in Paris comprising a vast property stretching from Boulevard de Port-Royal to Porte d'Orléans, with two houses, one in Rue de Lourcine and the other in the Tombe-Issoire area, beyond the former Saint-Jacques toll barrier. This area, occupied since very ancient times, became known as 'Tumbe Ysoré', after the tomb of the mythical giant Ysoré who terrorised local inhabitants.

The large building-stone quarries there began by extracting the upper Lutetian limestone, then, after 1450, on a second level lower down in the middle Lutetian, stone identical to that extracted from quarries in the Oise Valley at less expense.

Quarrying techniques

To extract stone underground, quarrymen always had to leave the uppermost layer of rock in place to form the quarry roof or 'sky'.

In the quarry galleries, stone was extracted from the cutting face in two successive phases. The first, called 'souchevage', consisted in cutting out a horizontal trench in the 'souchet', the thin layer of softer stone separating each strata of limestone. This was done with a two-pointed pickaxe called an 'esse'.

The second operation, called 'défermage', consisted in vertically cutting through one or several strata, sometimes through the entire height of the cutting face.

Iron wedges were then hammered into the trench to detach and bring down the block. The sides of the extracted blocks were given a 'first cut' to comply with the dimensions required by the client.

The finished stones were then loaded on a cart, taken out of the quarry via the gallery mouth and transported through the city streets to the construction site.

In the 14th century, the use of extraction pits became more frequent. The stone was manually pushed to the foot of the shaft on wooden rollers, where it was raised using a large wheel with ladder rungs around its rim. The weight of a man climbing these rungs turned the wheel, winding the cable and lifting the stone.

fig. 22
Quarrying limestone in an underground quarry at Bagneux: quarrymen cutting out a 'souchevage', 1906.

Paris stone

From the 1st century AD, Lutetia was graced with major monuments, including a forum, theatre, amphitheatre and baths. The nearby open-air quarries could no longer provide enough dimension stone, so the Parisian bargemen who controlled river traffic on the Seine and its tributaries brought 'Oise stone' (Lutetian limestone) from Pontoise and Creil. In the period of invasions, instability and recession that followed the fall of the Western Roman Empire, stone constructions became rare.

fig. 23
Splitting stone underground before it is raised to the surface via a lifting shaft, 1906.

From the 11th to the 13th century, Paris's demographic and economic growth transformed it into one of the largest cities in medieval Europe. To meet increasing demand, stone soon had to be extracted underground. Paris's stone, renowned for its quality, was widely exported along the Seine River.

From the mid-14th century to the 19th century, underground extraction using shafts made Paris stone very expensive, and 'Oise stone', and to a lesser extent the easier to extract stone from Vernon (Eure) and Château-Landon (Seine-et-Marne), began to arrive in Paris in great quantity by boat.

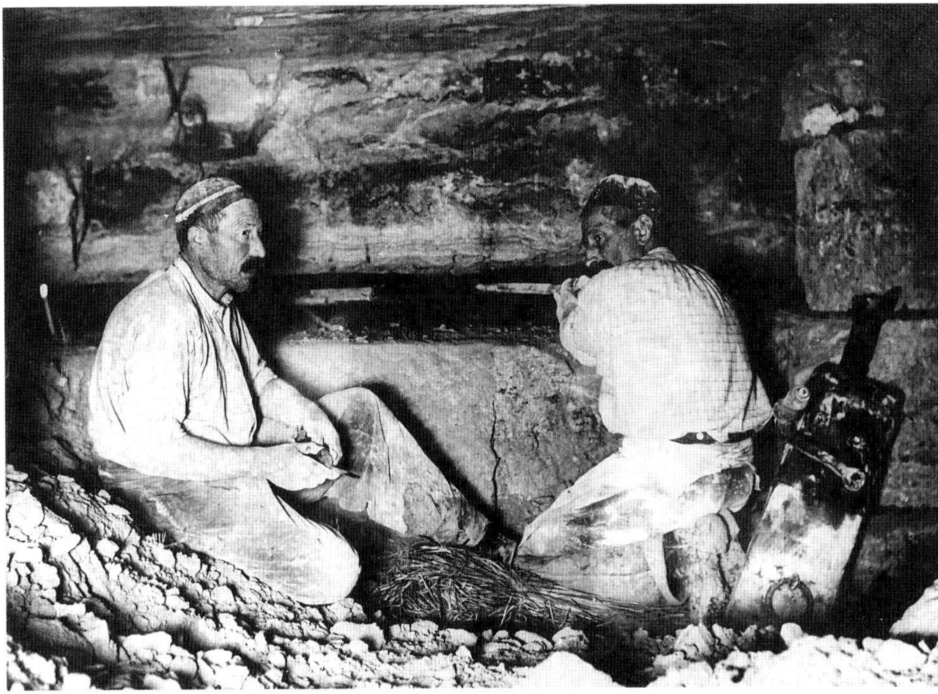

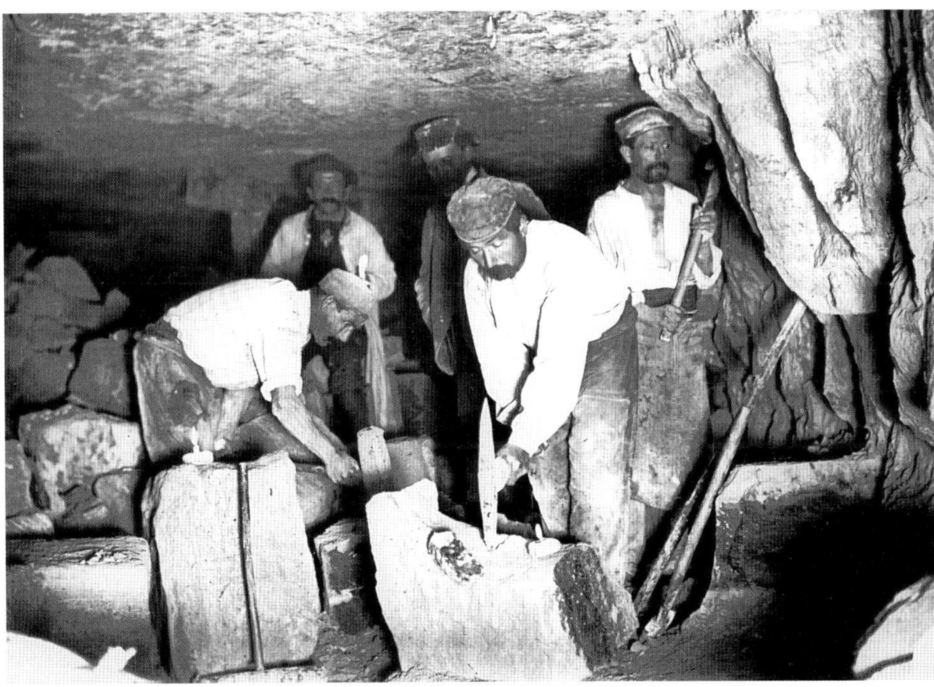

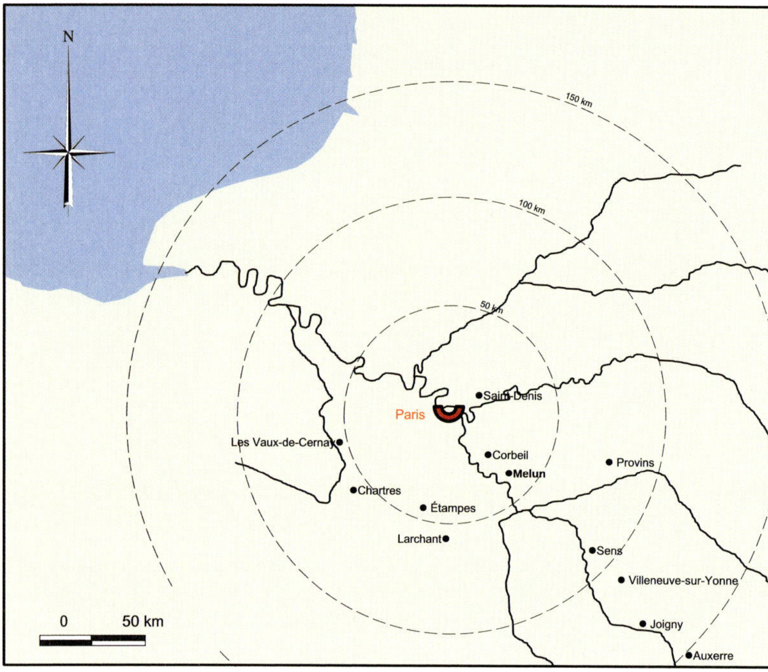

fig. 24
Map of the use of Paris stone in the 13th century.
This stone became the material par excellence for majestic Gothic constructions such as the Basilica of Saint-Denis and Notre-Dame de Paris.

Yet high-quality Paris stone, such as *cliquart* and *liais,* continued to be extracted from the many underground quarries in the capital's southern suburbs. From the 1850s onwards, the importation of stone from Burgundy, Poitou and the Meuse Valley by rail turned the stone market upside down. The extraction of Lutetian limestone in Paris's suburbs ended after the First World War, but high quality construction stone continues to be extracted in the Oise Valley and exported all over the world.

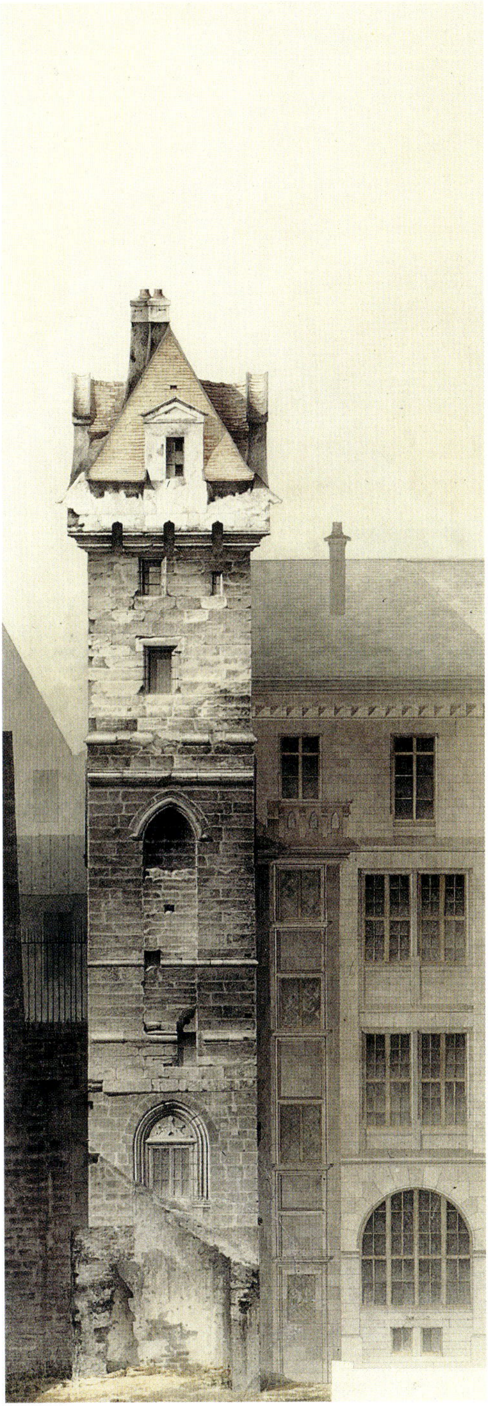

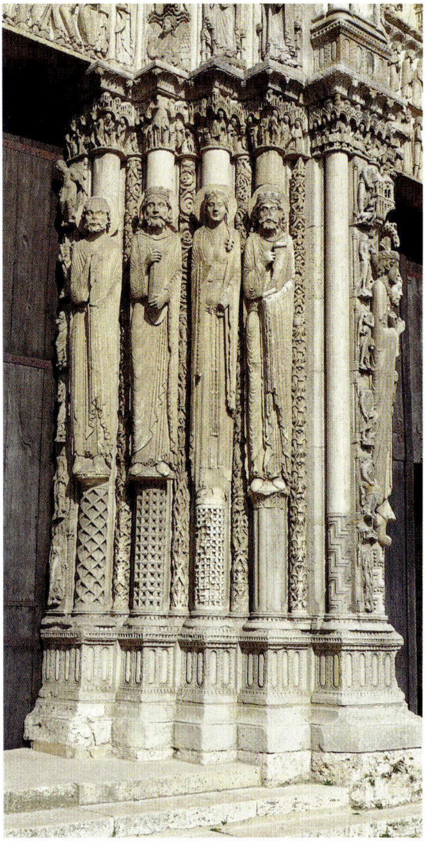

fig. 25
The Tour Jean-sans-Peur, 20 Rue Étienne-Marcel (2nd arrondissement), right lateral façade, 1877. Drawing by Jean Huillard, Musée Carnavalet, Paris. This tower was part of the residence of the dukes of Burgundy. It was built with fine Parisian *cliquart* and *liais franc* limestone in the first decade of the 15th century.

fig. 26
Portal of the western façade of Chartres Cathedral, built with Parisian *cliquart* and *liais franc* limestone.

The state of the Parisian quarries in the 18th century: a forgotten subterranean world

In the 16th and 17th centuries, exploitation of the quarries on the Left Bank in Paris continued at Saint-Germain-des-Prés and Vaugirard, and in the faubourgs of Saint-Jacques, Saint-Victor and Saint-Marcel. During Louis XV's reign, the surface area of the quarries beneath modern Paris increased to a tenth of the city's area.

When quarries were no longer exploitable, their pits were filled in and they were closed and gradually forgotten. The result was a vast subterranean labyrinth unknown to the world on the surface.

François Mansart took stock of the situation when he began the construction of the abbey of Val-de-Grâce in

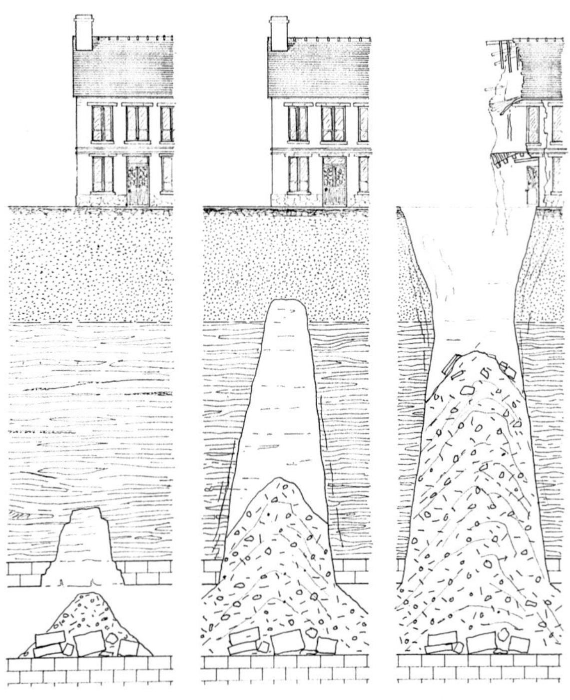

fig. 27
Formation of a 'fontis': as the quarry ceiling progressively collapses, the bell-shaped cavity it leaves rises through the more fragile layers of pebbles and clay.

1645, undertaking enormous consolidations before beginning construction. This wise precaution was deemed unnecessary, he was criticised for the project's slow progress and cost and another architect was appointed to replace him. Claude Perrault used the same technique to build the Observatory. But apart from these two exceptional building projects, nobody paid any heed to abandoned quarries beneath, because until then subsidences had only taken place on farm and garden land. Not until several spectacular accidents in the late 18th century did awareness of the dangers posed by the honeycombed network of quarries beneath the capital become more acute.

The creation of the General Inspectorate of Quarries

The former gypsum quarries in north and east Paris and the Lutetian limestone quarries in the south and west began to pose serious security problems. On 30 April 1772, an initial police order demanded a report on their state and a map of their extent. In 1774, Count d'Angiviller, director-general of the Bâtiments du Roi, had the renowned architects Jacques-Germain Soufflot, Maximilien Brébion and Charles-Axel Guillaumot visit the disused quarries beneath the Val-de-Grâce and the Observatory. On 4 April 1777, he had Louis XVI establish the Council of a quarries service for Paris and the surrounding plains, the present-day General Inspectorate of Quarries (IGC).

Guillaumot, architect of the Intendancy of Paris was appointed as its director. His mission was threefold: to draw up plans of all accessible quarries, to consolidate all roads and public spaces, and oblige property owners to do likewise.

As soon as he took up office in 1777, he had to deal with several major quarry subsidences, in Rue d'Enfer, near the Luxembourg Palace, and at the entrance to the village of Vaugirard, on the corner of the present-day Rue Bargue and Rue de Vaugirard (15th arrondissement). A decision made by Paris's parliament states that close watch had to be kept over 'everything concerning the existence of the quarries, at a distance of one league from the outskirts of Paris, and even further afield on terrain where there may be quarries'.

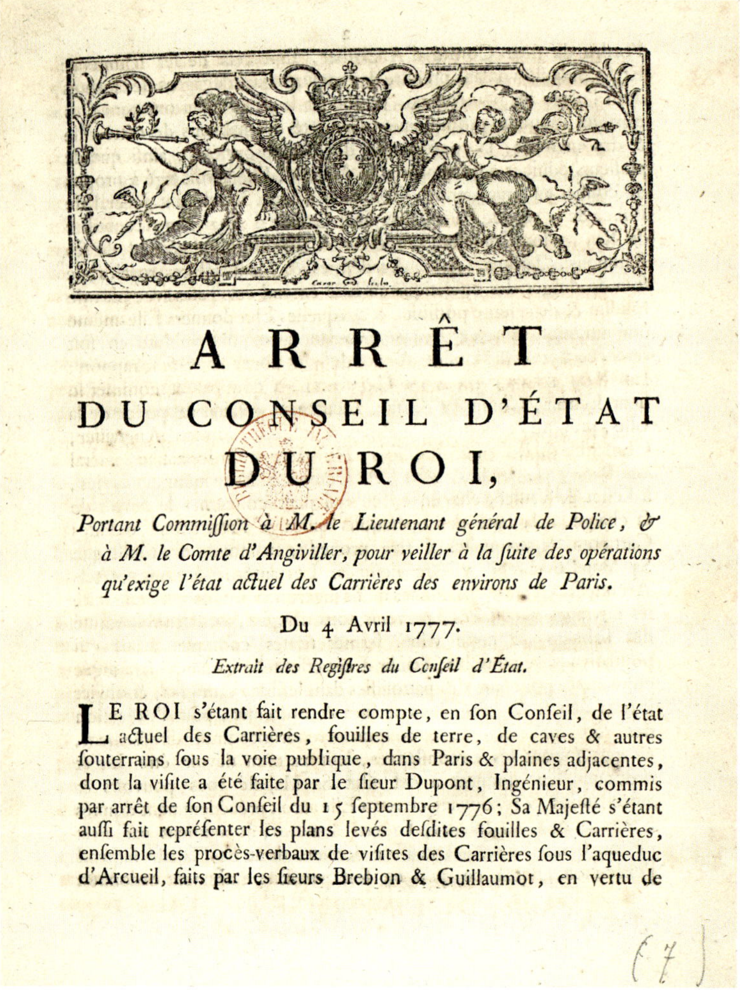

ARRÊT
DU CONSEIL D'ÉTAT DU ROI,

Portant Commiſſion à M. le Lieutenant général de Police, & à M. le Comte d'Angiviller, pour veiller à la ſuite des opérations qu'exige l'état actuel des Carrières des environs de Paris.

Du 4 Avril 1777.

Extrait des Regiſtres du Conſeil d'État.

LE ROI s'étant fait rendre compte, en ſon Conſeil, de l'état actuel des Carrières, fouilles de terre, de caves & autres ſouterrains ſous la voie publique, dans Paris & plaines adjacentes, dont la viſite a été faite par le ſieur Dupont, Ingénieur, commis par arrêt de ſon Conſeil du 15 ſeptembre 1776; Sa Majeſté s'étant auſſi fait repréſenter les plans levés deſdites fouilles & Carrières, enſemble les procès-verbaux de viſites des Carrières ſous l'aqueduc d'Arcueil, faits par les ſieurs Brebion & Guillaumot, en vertu de

(7)

fig. 28
Decision of the King's Council, 4 April 1777.

A contemporary testimony

Shortly before the Revolution, Louis-Sébastien Mercier published *Tableau de Paris*, a precise, picturesque portrait of the city in which he recounts the anxieties caused by unstable quarry galleries and fear of subsidences.

'It is an underground city, with its streets, crossroads and squares. One looks at the ground, higher here, lower there, and when one sees fissures and one reflects on what part of this superb city rests, a shiver runs up one's spine and one dreads the action of centripetal force. Cavities, half-broken ceilings, subsidences that have not yet reached the surface, pillars that have collapsed under the weight bearing down on them and threaten disaster, double quarries, on which precariously rest the pillars of the first [two-storey underground quarry]; what a list. And one eats, drinks and sleeps in the edifices resting on this precarious crust.

[...]

But this is not so since this work was entrusted to the Bâtiments du Roi: the first system adopted was the repairing of the roadways; the more endangered, the more they are dealt with.'

Louis-Sébastien Mercier, *Tableau de Paris* (Paris: Éd. Amsterdam, 1782) vol. 1, chapter 189, 'Plancher d'une partie de la capitale', pp. 463–64.

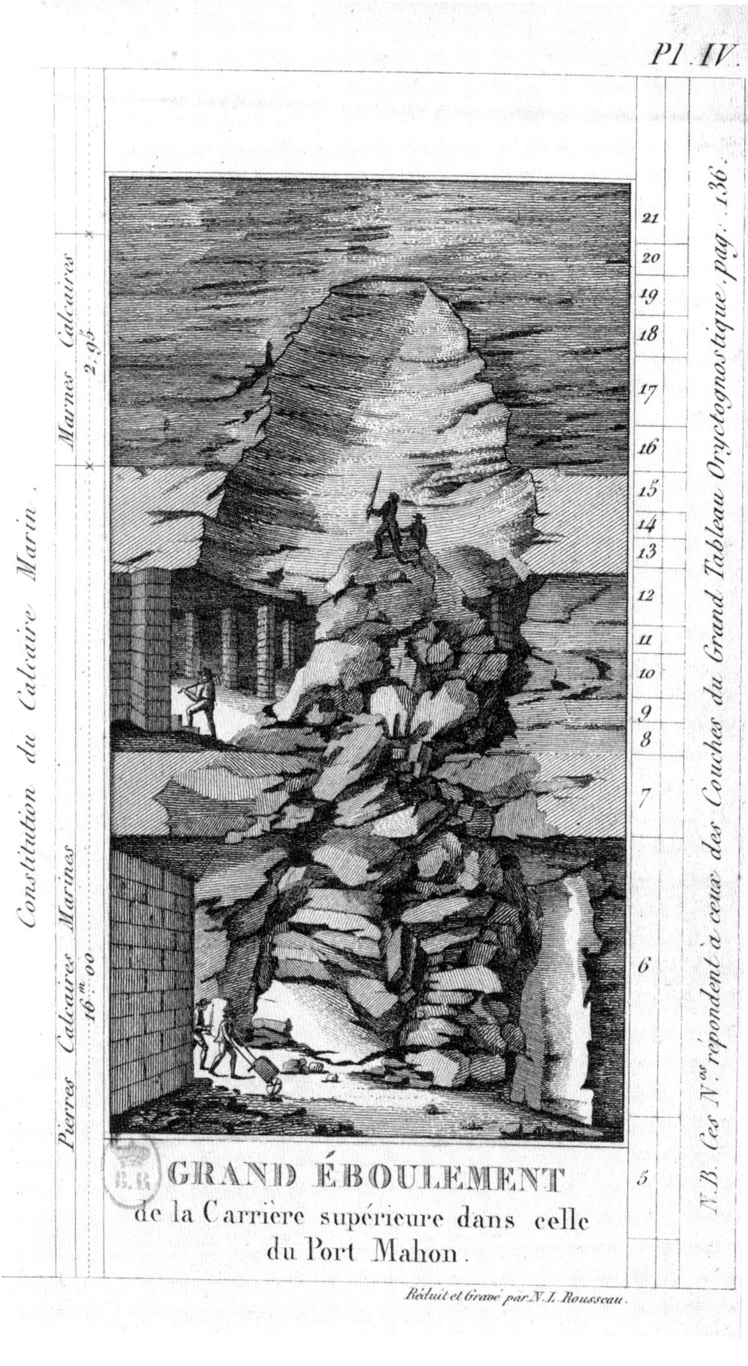

fig. 29
View of a 'fontis' (subsidence cavity) and the collapse of the Mont-Souris quarry into the Port-Mahon quarry. Louis-Étienne François Héricart de Thury, *Description des Catacombes de Paris*, pl. IV, 1815.

> fig. 30
The collapse of a house caused by a 'fontis' above the Catacombs in passage Gourdon Daniel Urrabieta Ortiz y Vierge, known as Daniel Vierge (1851–1904).

> fig. 31
Subsidence occasionally occurred the 20th century. In July 1929, part of the roadway spectacularly disappeared in Rue Pierre-Larousse in Malakoff (Hauts-de-Seine).

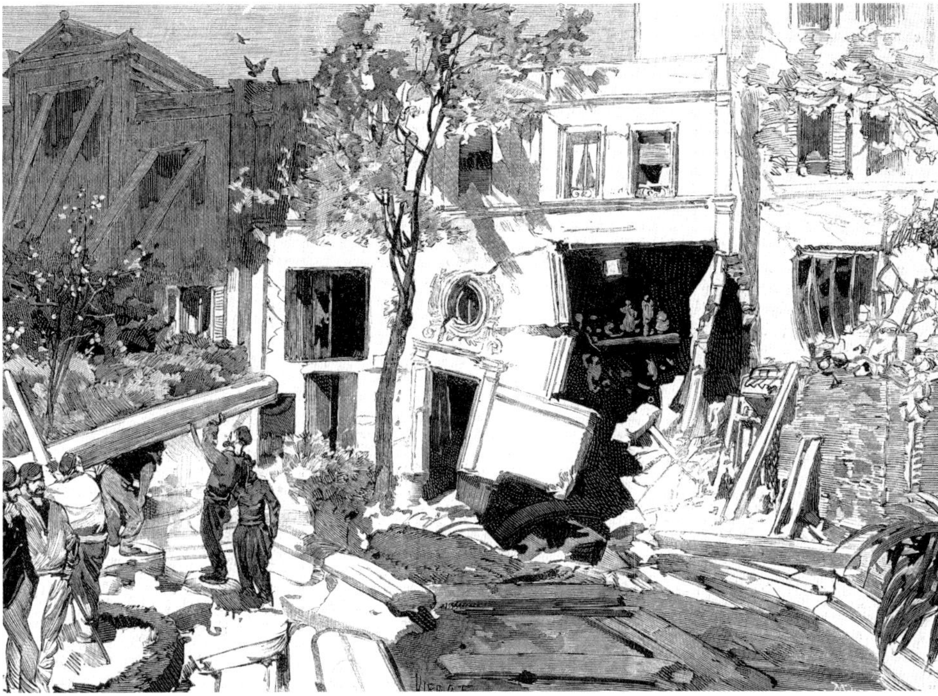

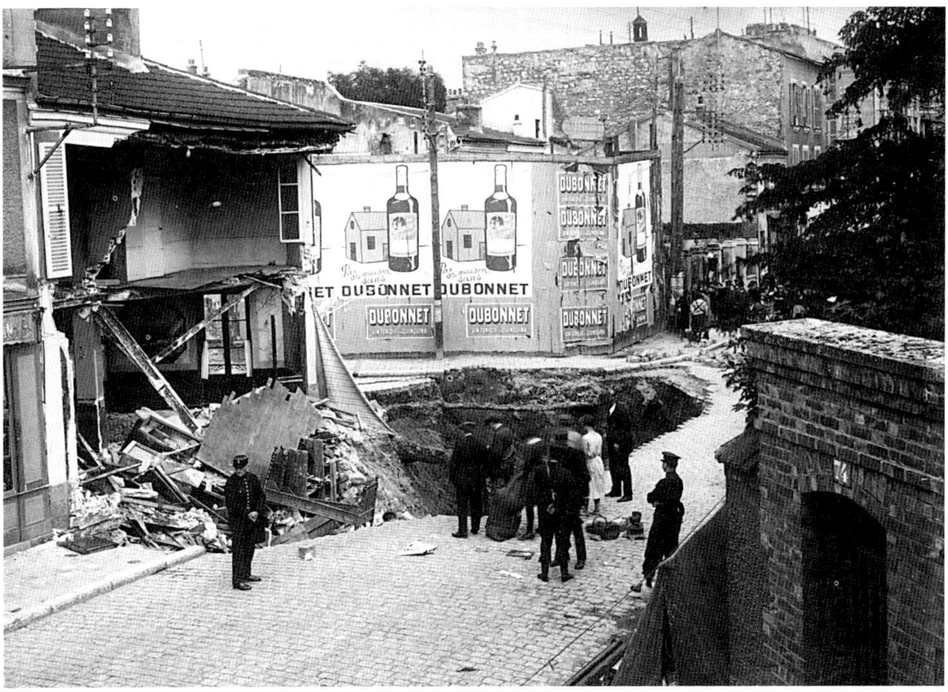

RET DUBONNET
DUBONNET
DUBONNET
DUBONNET
DUBONNET
DUBONNET
DUBONNET
DUBONNET

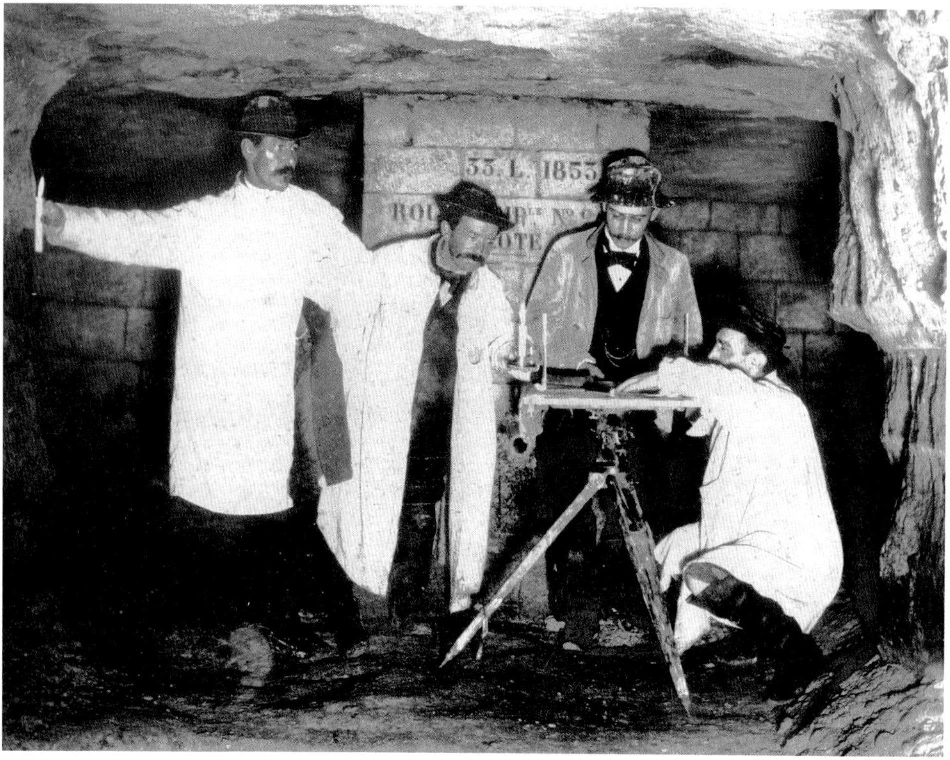

Refurbishments and consolidations

To consolidate streets, Guillaumot devised a system of 'service galleries' that traversed the quarry voids beneath. Comprising two rows of masonry pillars, these galleries were built beneath the façades on either side of the street. They were regularly joined by transversal galleries, and when they encountered quarry pillars these were hollowed through and traversed. Empty spaces were identified on a map then carefully filled in. Each masonry pillar bore its number and construction date. Each gallery was identified by a plaque bearing the name of the project or the street above. This underground network soon became known as 'the lining Paris'.

fig. 32
In the early 20th century, surveyors drew up maps of all the disused underground quarries in Paris and the suburbs

A similar principle was adopted for the Marie de Médicis aqueduct, which fed the fountains in the Luxembourg Gardens, with the construction of a continuous wall of masonry beneath the aqueduct, flanked by two parallel galleries.

During this work, in May 1781, a 'fontis', 20 metres in diameter, opened in the plain, swallowing up part of the aqueduct and depriving the fountains of water. Guillaumot had to entirely rebuild a 150-metre-long section of the aqueduct along a different route avoiding other subsidences. The consolidations and service galleries in the adjacent quarries were created at the same time.

fig. 33
Entrance XXV to the Médicis aqueduct, Avenue René-Coty.

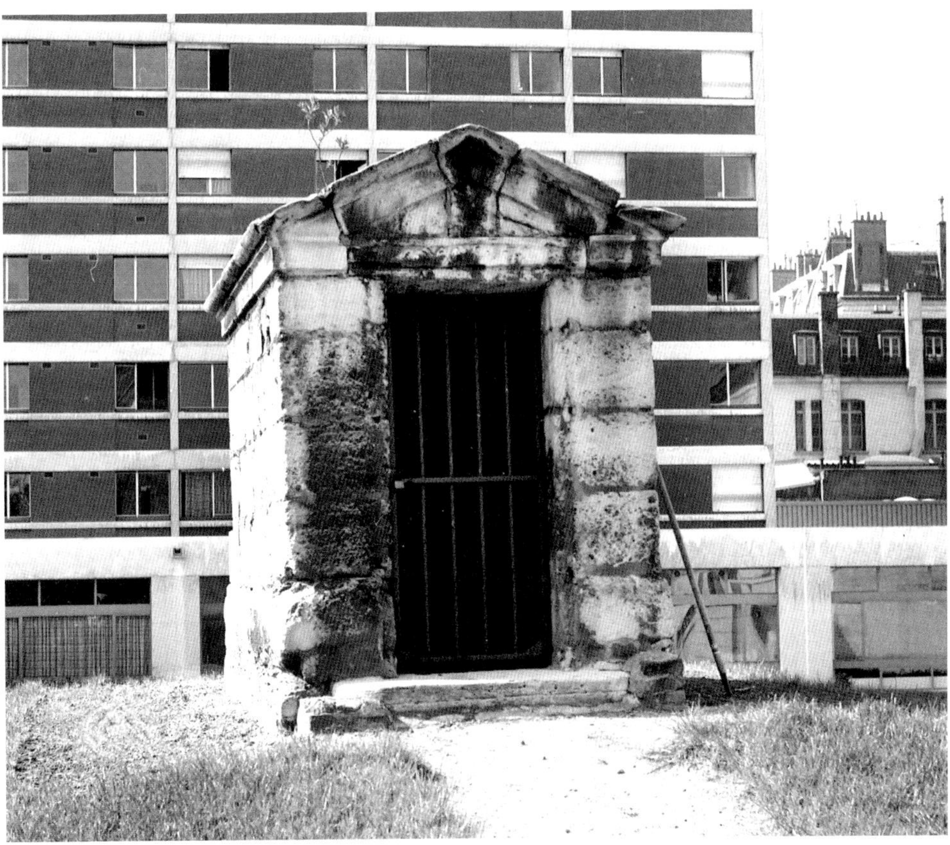

Underground signage

The architects and engineers of the General Inspectorate of Quarries signed their subterranean constructions, engraving their initials and the construction number and date in the stone. Thus one can follow the chronology and topography of the work undertaken, including consolidations of quarry pillars and ceilings, filling in of subsidence cavities and restructuring of empty spaces.

The underground galleries form a labyrinth more than 250 kilometres long. With the creation of the General Inspectorate of Quarries, the abandoned quarries beneath Paris became an organised, constructed subterranean urban territory, where it was possible to get your bearing thanks to the plaques giving the names of the streets above.

fig. 34
Inscription beneath entrance XXV to the Médicis aqueduct indicating the 13th consolodation of Charles-Axel Guillaumot in 1783.

fig. 35
Inscription engraved by Charles-Axel Guillaumot on the 74th consolidation in 1780.

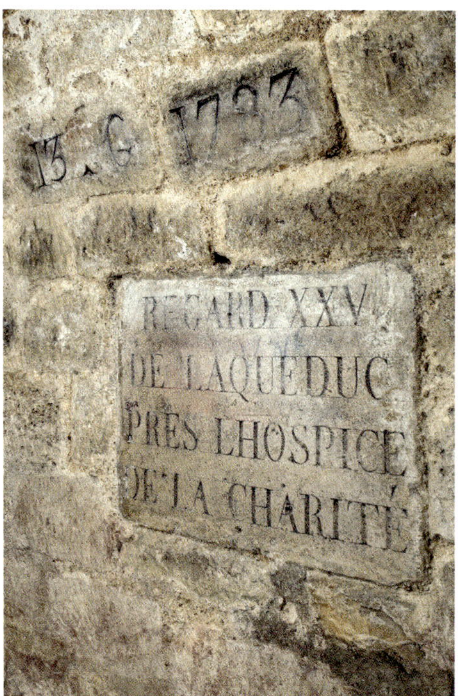

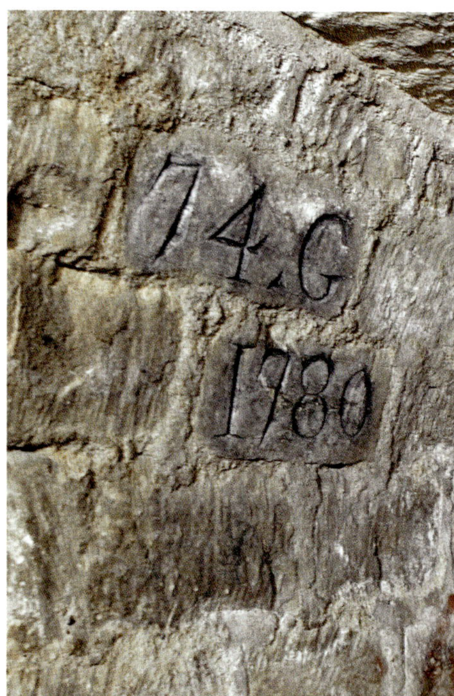

fig. 36
Inscription on a 'turned pillar' under the Arcueil aqueduct (also called the Médicis aqueduct).

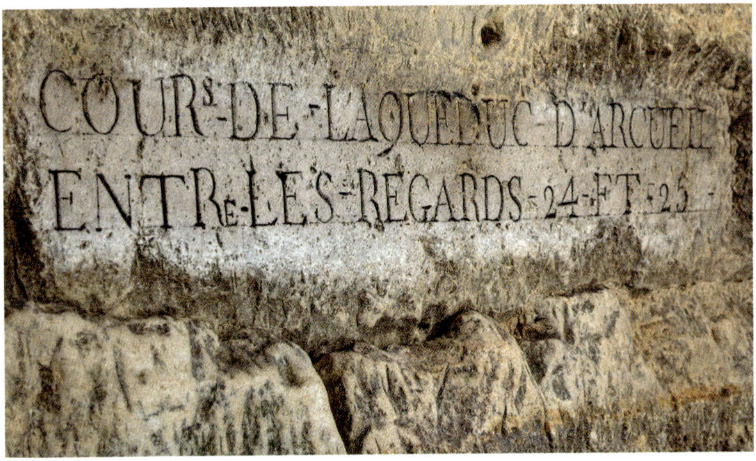

fig. 37
Plaine de Mont Souris.

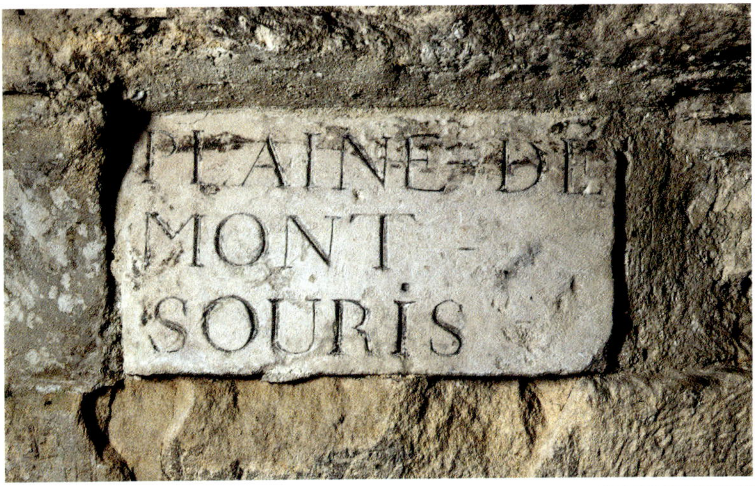

fig.38
Rue Hallé.

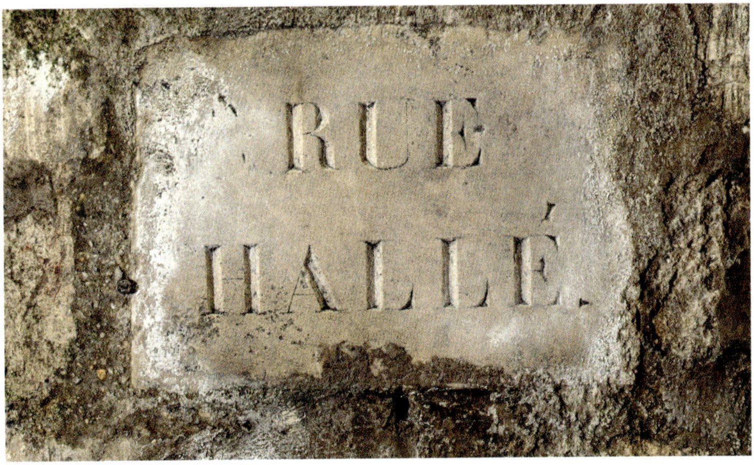

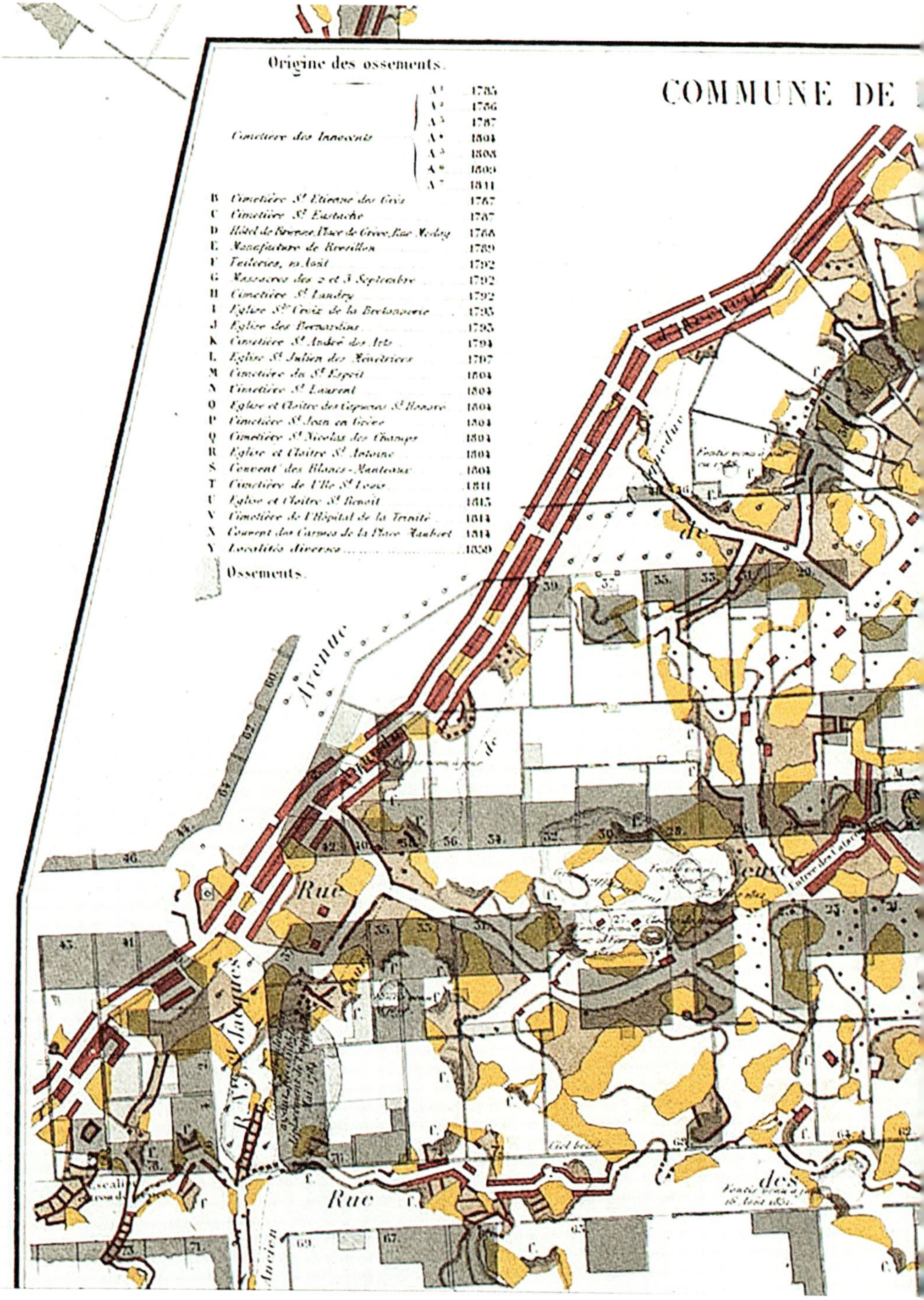
Origine des ossements.
Cimetière des Innocents A¹ 1785
A² 1786
A³ 1787
A⁴ 1804
A⁵ 1808
A⁶ 1809
A⁷ 1811
B Cimetière St Etienne des Grès 1787
C Cimetière St Eustache 1787
D Hôtel de Brienne, Place de Grève, Rue Meslay 1788
E Manufacture de Reveillon 1789
F Tuileries, en Août 1792
G Massacres des 2 et 3 Septembre 1792
H Cimetière St Landry 1792
I Eglise Ste Croix de la Bretonnerie 1793
J Eglise des Bernardins 1793
K Cimetière St André des Arts 1794
L Eglise St Julien des Ménétriers 1797
M Cimetière du St Esprit 1804
N Cimetière St Laurent 1804
O Eglise et Cloître des Capucins St Honoré 1804
P Cimetière St Jean en Grève 1804
Q Cimetière St Nicolas des Champs 1804
R Eglise et Cloître St Antoine 1804
S Couvent des Blancs-Manteaux 1804
T Cimetière de l'Ile St Louis 1811
U Eglise et Cloître St Benoît 1813
V Cimetière de l'Hôpital de la Trinité 1814
X Couvent des Carmes de la Place Maubert 1814
Y Localités diverses 1830
Ossements.
COMMUNE DE
Avenue
Rue
Rue
des

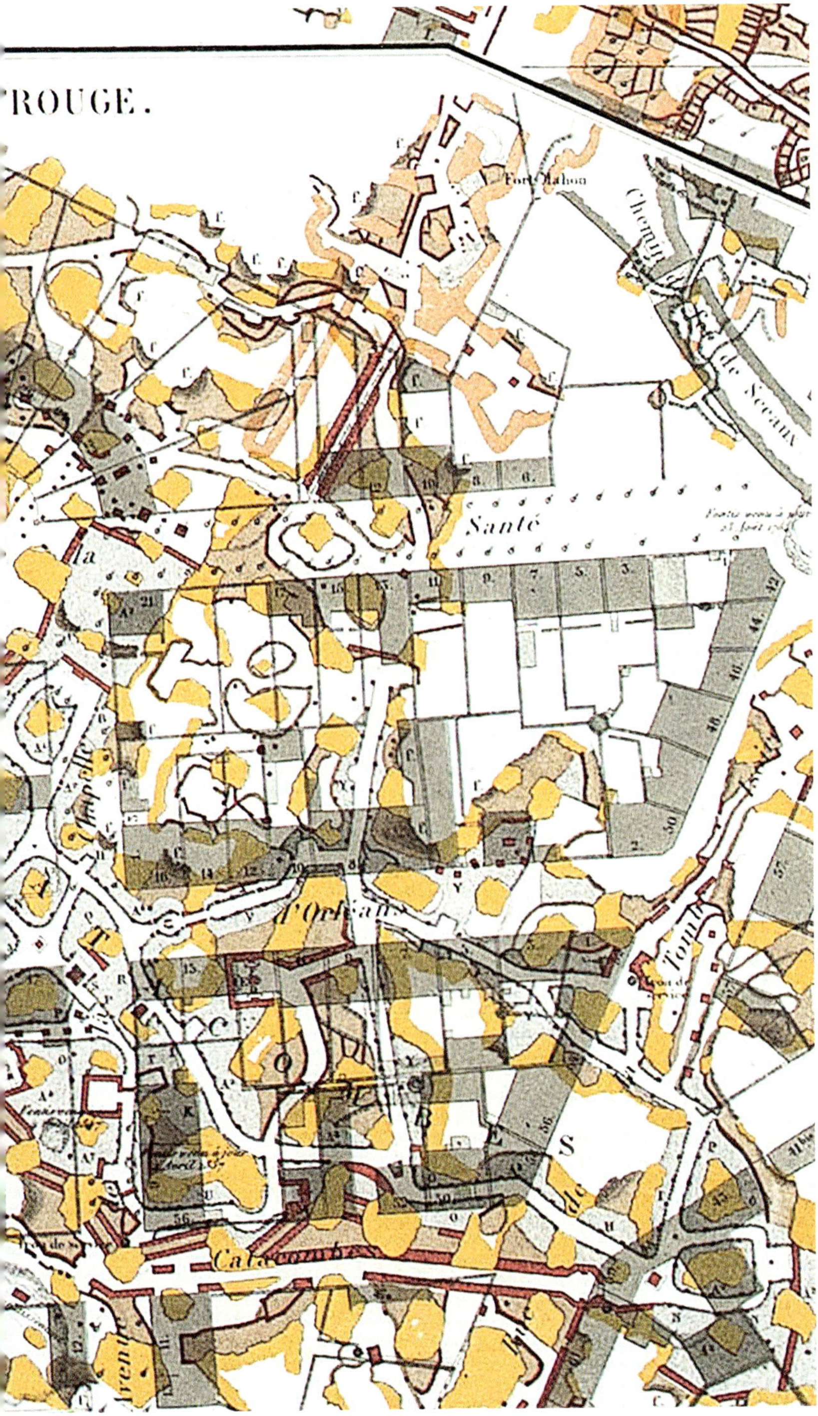

fig. 39
Plan indicating the pillars of the medieval quarry in yellow and the reinforcement masonry in red. Eugène de Fourcy (1812–1889), *Atlas souterrain de la ville de Paris*, 1859–60.

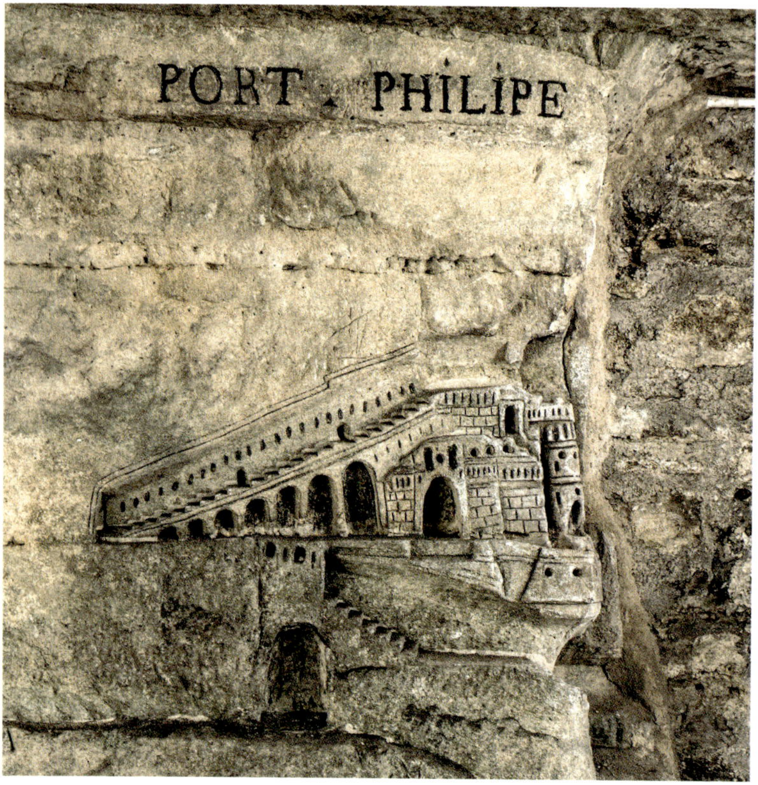

fig. 40
Port-Mahon, Fort Saint-Philippe sculpture, by Décure. Some parts were sculpted in the rock face and others were added.

The sculptures by Décure

The sculptures in the Port-Mahon gallery are one of the most unexpected curiosities in the Catacombs. Created before the site's transformation into an ossuary, they were integrated new underground planning. They were created by Décure, nicknamed Beauséjour, who worked on the consolidation of the Tombe-Issoire quarries under the directorship of Charles-Axel Guillaumot, after a subsidence destroyed one floor of the gallery in 1777. At intervals during his daily work, Décure worked alone in an atelier, on the quarry's lower level, carving these high-relief reproductions of the fortresses of Maó-Mahón on the island of Menorca into the limestone. A veteran of Louis XV's army, he had been stationed at Maó-Mahón during the Seven Years War between the French, allies of the Spanish, and the English for the possession of the Balearic Islands. Although not precisely identified, the sculpted elements are probably depictions of the fortifications at Maó-Mahón.

The surrounding pavement of black flint set in lime mortar, laid before the sculptures, is still visible today. When he had finished the sculptures in 1782, Décure tried to create a direct access to the level above, ironically prompting a collapse that killed him. Guillaumot had a plaque installed in his memory.

Use of the quarry's empty spaces

At the end of the Ancien Régime it became impossible to force private owners to consolidate their property. In 1810, the new Civil Code clarified things: in France, ownership of land included the ground beneath it to the centre of the Earth. Yet paradoxically landowners did not own the minerals (iron ore, coal) extracted by mining beneath their property.

Agronomists and industrialists were quick to take advantage of this. In 1819, the agronomist Chambry successfully grew mushrooms in the abandoned quarries beneath Rue de la Santé, and Paris mushrooms became well known.

Another 'by-product' of the quarries was brewing. In the late 18th century, several brewers began producing beer in the old medieval quarries between Rue de la Santé and Rue de la Tombe-Issoire. The most famous of these was the Brasserie de l'Empereur, founded at 22 Rue Dareau (14th arrondissement) during the First Empire.

But the growth in construction throughout the 19th century eventually forced these subterranean mushroom growers and brewers out into the suburbs. The construction of large stone buildings during the Second Empire and the 3rd Republic changed this. These buildings were much heavier than the old houses in Paris's faubourgs, and consolidating the quarries was made compulsory by a decree issued by the Prefect of the Seine, Eugène Poubelle, on 18 January 1881.

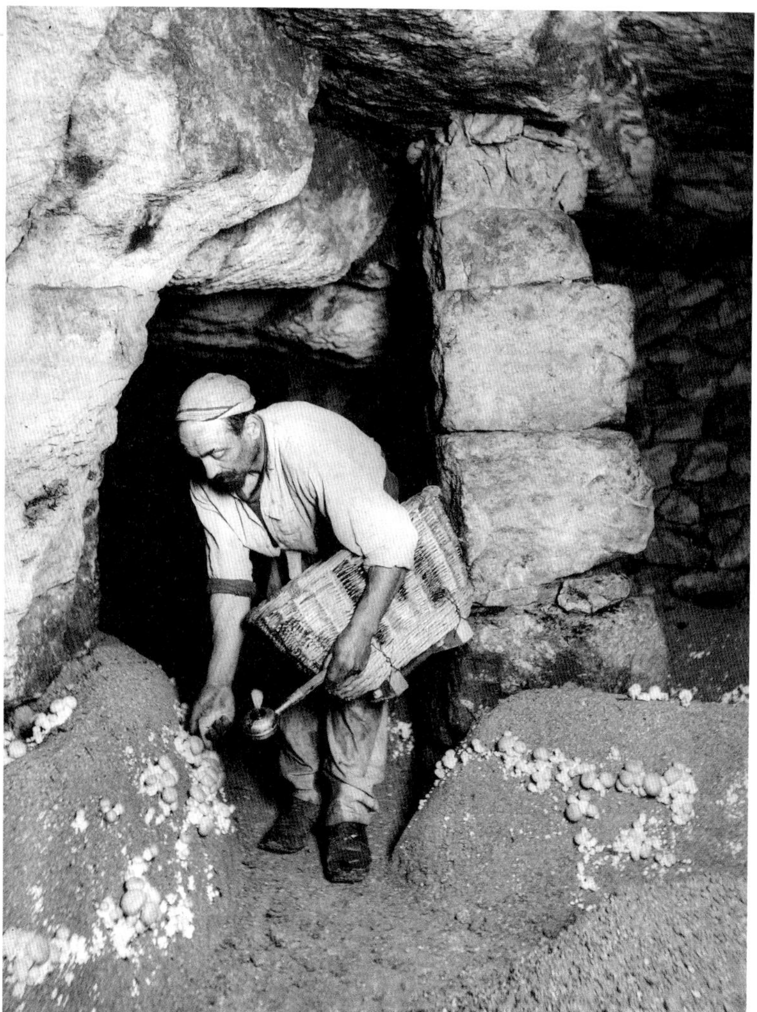

fig. 41
Harvesting Paris mushrooms around 1900. Mushrooms do not need light to grow, and could therefore be cultivated on extraction rubble in underground quarries.

FROM QUARRY TO OSSUARY

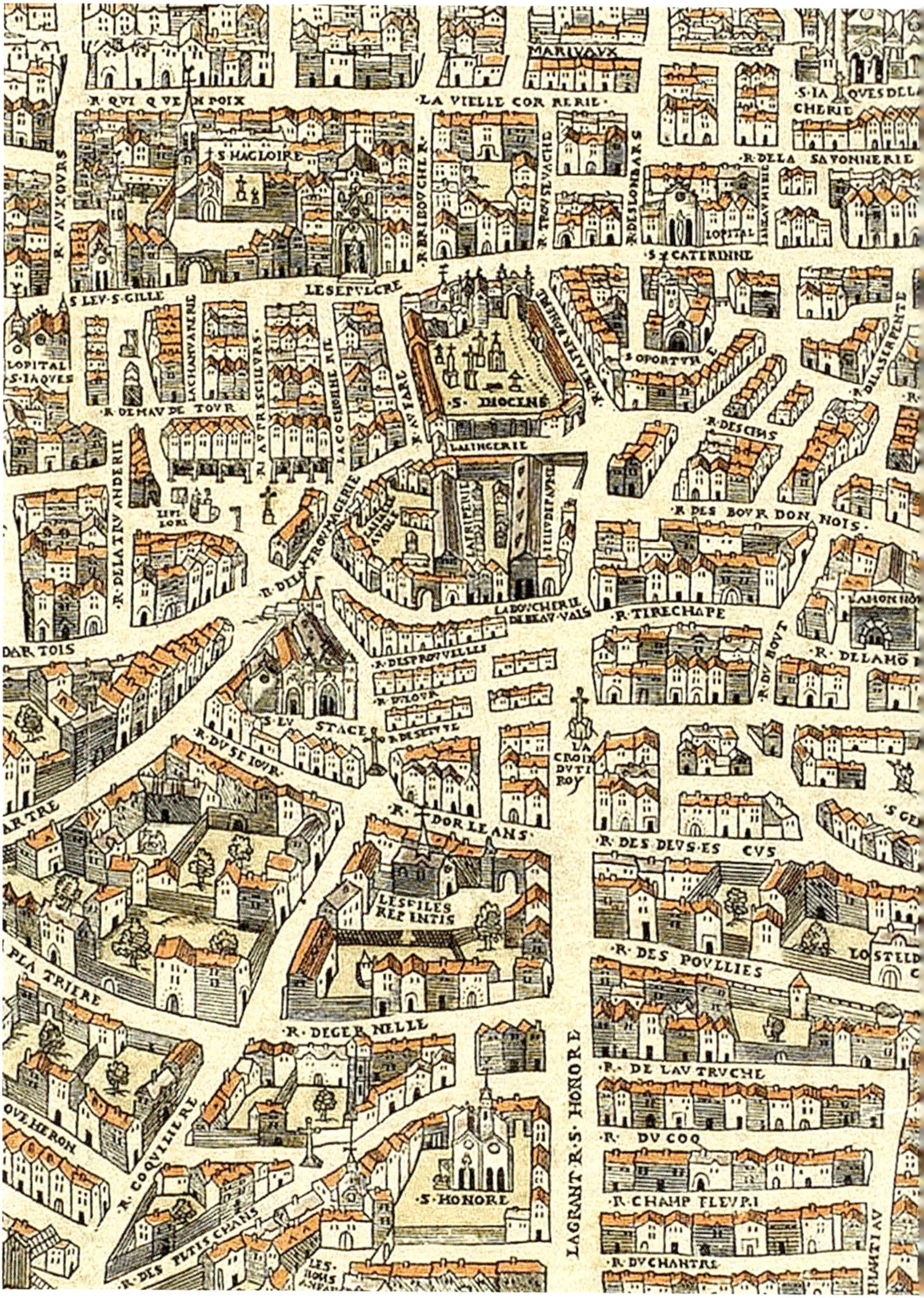
MARIVAUX
LA VIELLE COR RERIE
S. MAGLOIRE
R. DELA SAVONNERIE
LOPITAL
S. CATERINNE
LE SEPVLCRE
S. LEV. S. GILLE
LOPITAL S. IAQVES
R. DEMAVDE TOVR
LALINGERIE
R. DES BOVR DON NOIS
R. TIRECHAPE
LA BOVCHERIE DE BEAV VAIS
DARTOIS
R. DV SEIOVR
LA CROIX DV TI ROY
R. DORLEANS
R. DES DEVS ES CVS
LES FILES REPENTIS
R. DES POVLLIES
PLA TRIERE
R. DEGER NELLE
R. DE LAVTRVCHE
R. DV COQ
S. HONORE
R. CHAMP FLEVRI
R. DV CHANTRE
LAGRANT R. S. HONORE
R. COQVILLIRE
R. DES PETIS CHANS

Paris cemeteries in the late 18th century

fig. 42
Map of Paris, known as the 'plan de Bâle', 1551, Truschet and Hoyau. Detail showing the Cimetière des Innocents.

From the Middle Ages onwards, cemeteries developed on ecclesiastical land around parish churches. The growth of the city and the construction of two successive city walls enclosed these cemeteries within the capital, where overpopulation began to affect both the living and the dead.

In the 18th century, the cemeteries within the city began to preoccupy doctors who feared ground, water and air contamination, which, despite not yet understanding the mechanisms, they suspected played a role in the spread of illness. New means of protecting oneself from the 'miasma' established themselves, and to purify the air there was a return to the ancient custom of confining necropoli and polluting activities to the edge of the city.

Studies were undertaken by public health specialists such as Doctor Félix Vicq-d'Azir, who denounced the dangers of urban cemeteries and the risks of contagion posed by tombs. In 1781, the chemist and pharmacist Antoine-Alexis Cadet de Vaux wrote a memorandum for the Royal Academy of Sciences on the Cimetière des Innocents, and his new theories on the harmful nature of the site and its 'sulphurous air pollution complicated by miasmas or a kind of cadaverous gas'.

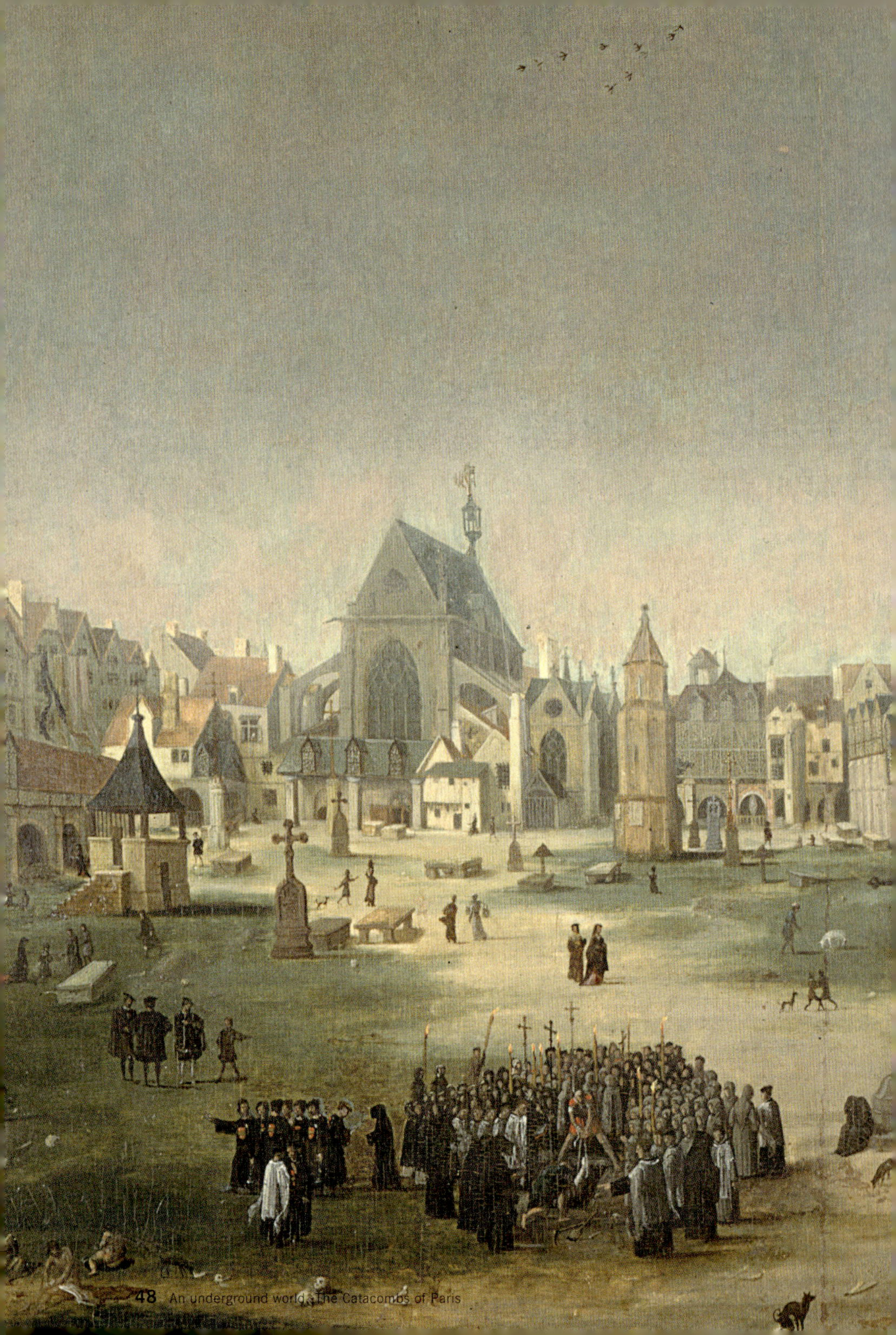

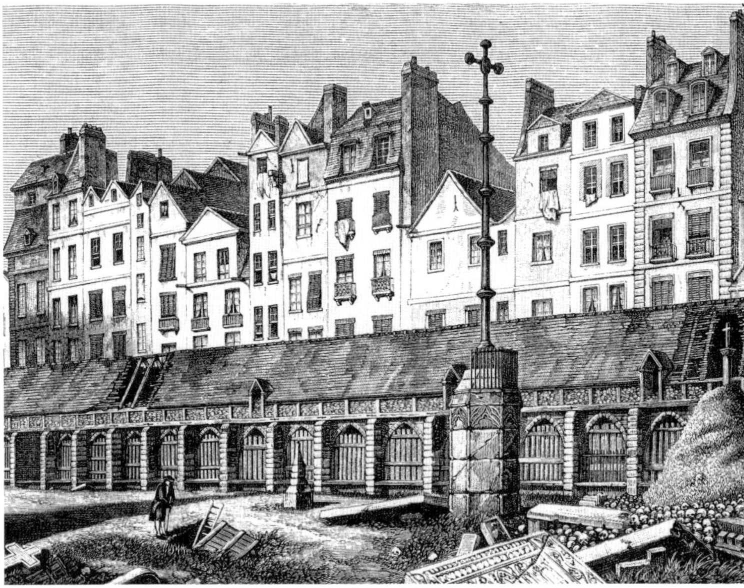

fig. 44
Mass graves in the Cimetière des Innocents. 19th-century engraving after a drawing by Charles-Louis Bernier, Musée Carnavalet, Paris. The presence of scattered bones recalls the chaotic state that prompted the cemetery's evacuation in the late 18th century.

The Cimetière des Saints-Innocents

The cemetery that grew around the Eglise des Saint-Innocents is attested in the 12th century. The discovery of plaster sarcophagi during excavations in 1973–74 could date its creation to the early Middle Ages, on a site known as Les Champeaux, beyond the city limits, outside the wall built by Philippe Auguste. In 1137, Paris's central market, Les Halles, was transferred to a neighbouring site. Due to this proximity, the cemetery became a convenient haunt for market-related activities such as prostitution and banditry. Pigs had to be prevented from unearthing corpses there. By order of the king, a high wall was built around the cemetery, lined on the inside by an arcaded gallery with attics above. This gallery housed the tombs of donors, and its attics were filled with bones from emptied communal graves, carefully arranged to ensure more room.

fig. 43
The cemetery and the Église des Innocents in Paris. Oil on wood, attributed to Jakob Grimer (1526–1589), Musée Carnavalet, Paris.
The gabled houses in Rue de la Ferronnerie are visible on the left and in Rue aux Fers (now Rue Berger).

Packed with communal graves and individual tombs, the Cimetière des Saints-Innocents was Paris's largest cemetery, serving some twenty parishes and also receiving those who died at the Hôtel Dieu and in the streets.

Its overcrowded state was acknowledged by all and it was blamed for strange occurrences – milk that mysteriously went bad and wine that that turned sour – yet many Parisians, the religious authorities and most of the members of Paris's parliament remained opposed to moving it. A grisly incident eventually sealed the cemetery's fate: the collapse of a cellar wall next to a communal grave poured hundreds of cadavers into the basement of a house in Rue de la Lingerie. The parliament ordered the closure of the Cimetière des Innocents on 1 December 1780.

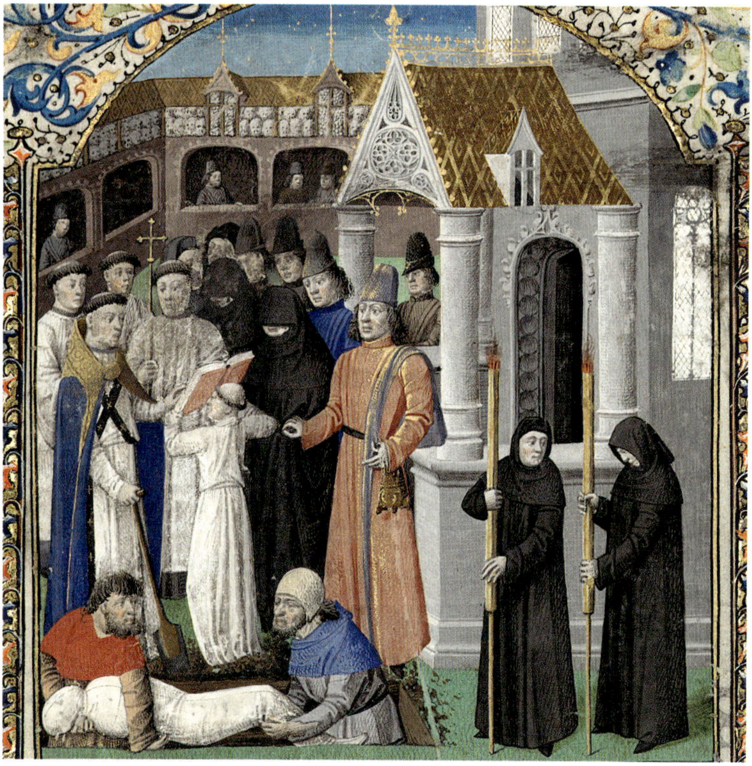

fig. 45
A burial in the Cimetière des Innocents around 1460. Miniature in *Heures de Notre-Dame*, Bibliothèque Nationale de France. The heaped bones are represented solely by naively depicted skulls.

fig. 46
Danse macabre, Le dit des trois morts et des trois vifs, Gillet Couteau and Jean Menard, 1492, Paris. Musée du Petit Palais, Paris.
The architectural designs separating the groups represent the stone arcades of the Cimetière des Innocents.

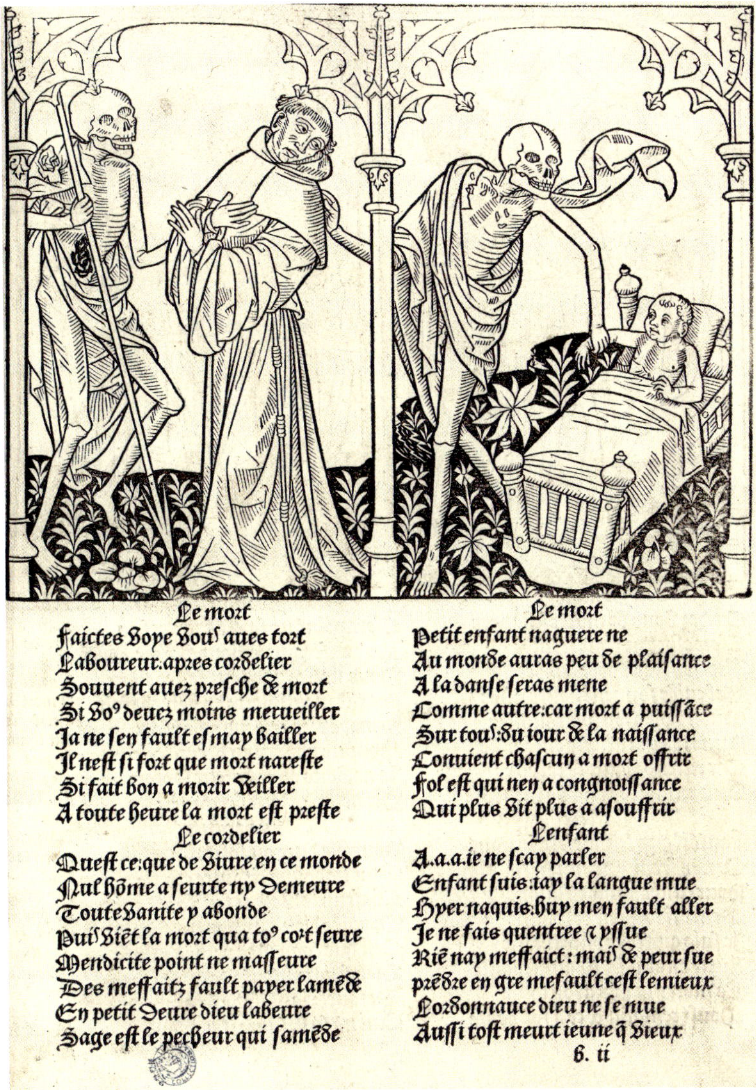

Le mort
Faictes voye vous aves tort
Laboureur: apres cordelier
Souuent auez presche de mort
Si vo⁹ deuez moins merueiller
Ja ne sen fault esmay bailler
Il nest si fort que mort nareste
Si fait bon a morir veiller
A toute heure la mort est preste

Le cordelier
Quest ce: que de viure en ce monde
Nul hôme a seurte ny demeure
Toute vanite y abonde
Puis viêt la mort qua to⁹ cort seure
Mendicite point ne masseure
Des meffaitz fault payer lamêde
En petit deure dieu labeure
Sage est le pecheur qui samêde

Le mort
Petit enfant naguere ne
Au monde auras peu de plaisance
A la danse seras mene
Comme autre: car mort a puissâce
Sur tous: du iour de la naissance
Conuient chascun a mort offrir
Fol est qui nen a congnoissance
Qui plus vit plus a a souffrir

Lenfant
A.a.a.ie ne scay parler
Enfant suis: iay la langue mue
Hyer naquis: huy men fault aller
Je ne fais quentree et yssue
Riê nay meffaict: mais de peur sue
prêdre en gre me fault cest le mieux
Lordonnauce dieu ne se mue
Aussi tost meurt ieune q̃ vieux
b. ii

The Dance of Death

The walls of the galleries were decorated with engraved epitaphs, sculptures and paintings. We know that in 1389 and 1407 Nicolas Flamel and his wife financed the construction of one of the arcades, in which a poem and religious inscriptions were engraved.

The South Gallery, known as the 'Writers' Gallery', was famously decorated with a 'Dance of Death'. Possibly the first representation of this subject in Europe, and probably painted in 1424–25, based on a text attributed to Jean Gerson, it became the prototype for depictions of the theme that we are all equal in death, regardless of our social status. Macabre cameos similar to mystery plays may also have been performed on a platform in front of the painting. The work's fame spread, and it is mentioned by Guillebert de Metz in *Description de la ville de Paris au XVe siècle*: 'Here in this place are notable paintings of the Dance of Death with scriptures to move people to worship.' In 1485, the publisher Guyot Marchant published *Le dit des trois morts et des trois vifs* (The Words of the Three Dead and the Three Living), in which the text of the Dance of Death is illustrated with engravings after the work in the Cimetère des Innocents. They bear testimony to the original paintings, destroyed in 1786, and show a dance in which Death is leading laymen, merchants, bourgeois, peasants and members of the clergy away in file.

The transfers of bones

The cemetery was definitively closed by order on 9 November 1785 and transformed into a public square. The doctor Michel Thouret, charged with disinfecting the site, noted that so many corpses were buried in the cemetery that the ground had risen some two metres higher than the adjacent streets. To sanitize the 3,600-square-metre site, he emptied more than eighty vaults and forty to fifty communal graves of around three metres deep. In all, 15,000 to 20,000 corpses out of the 90,000 estimated by Thouret, dating from all periods, were exhumed with their coffins.

The bishop finally gave his consent for their transfer, on the condition that 'the exhumation and exportation of all or some of the bones will be done only by night, with suitable decency and in carts closed at the bottom and on the sides and covered with canvas of the length and width of the said carts'.

Transferring the bones took six months, night and day, from December 1785 to May 1786. Each evacuation followed a certain staging, taking the form of a religious ceremony in the presence of priests and accompanied by a choir. The ritual ended on arrival, when the bones were unceremoniously tipped by the cartload into the quarry shafts and the shattered remains heaped at the end of the galleries.

Careful accounts were kept:

- 4,183 transports of bones;
- 1,568 transports of coffin wood;
- 11,898 transports of earth;
- 15,769 paper lanterns;
- 446 torches;
- 93 pounds of candles;
- 541 pounds of tar;
- 15 half-hogsheads of vinegar (the gravediggers were advised to carry a bottle of pure vinegar and sniff it from time to time);
- 19 hogsheads of lime;
- 384 ells of canvas;
- 51 pounds of solder.

In all: 17,129 days work by road workers and 2,266 days work by gravediggers.

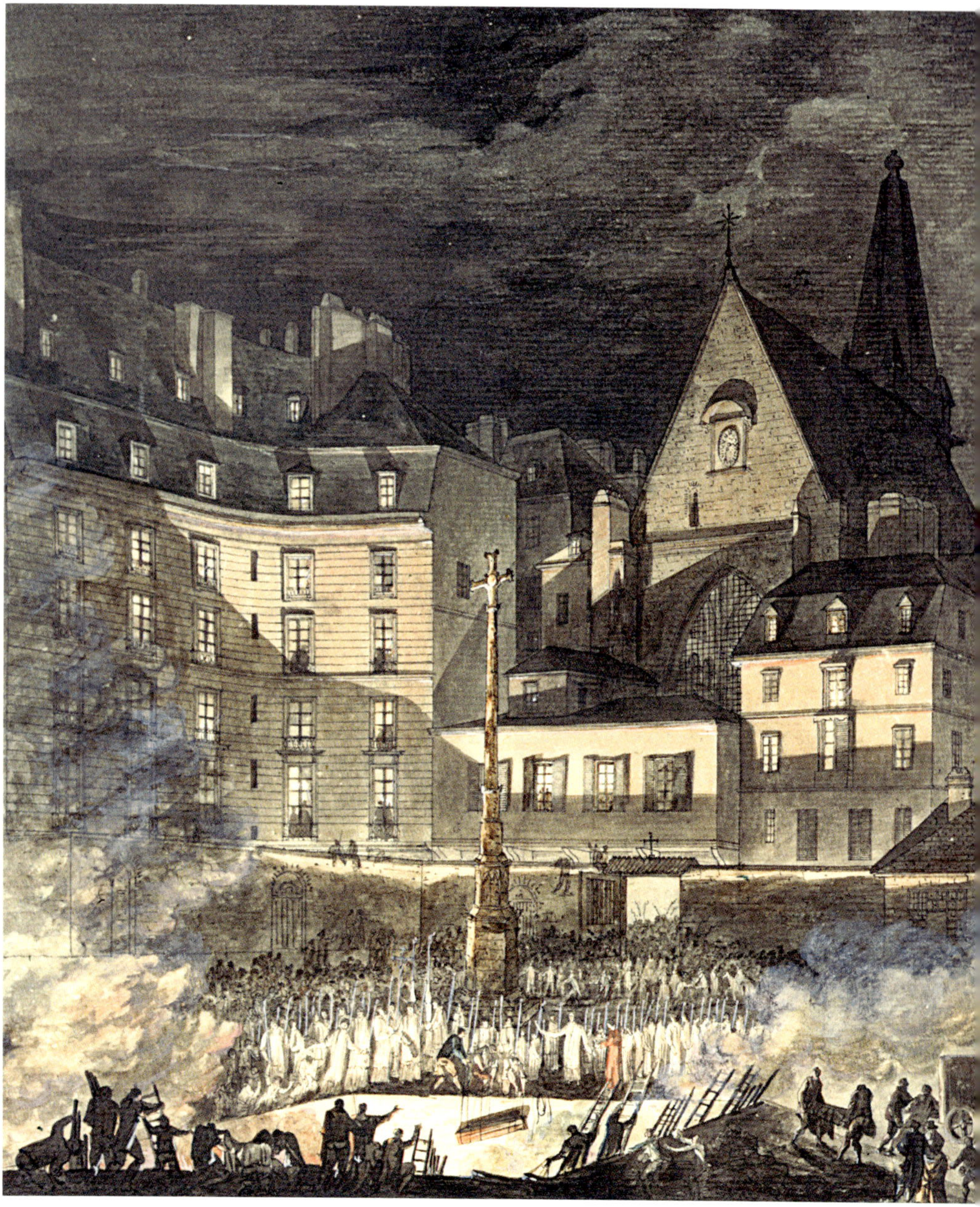

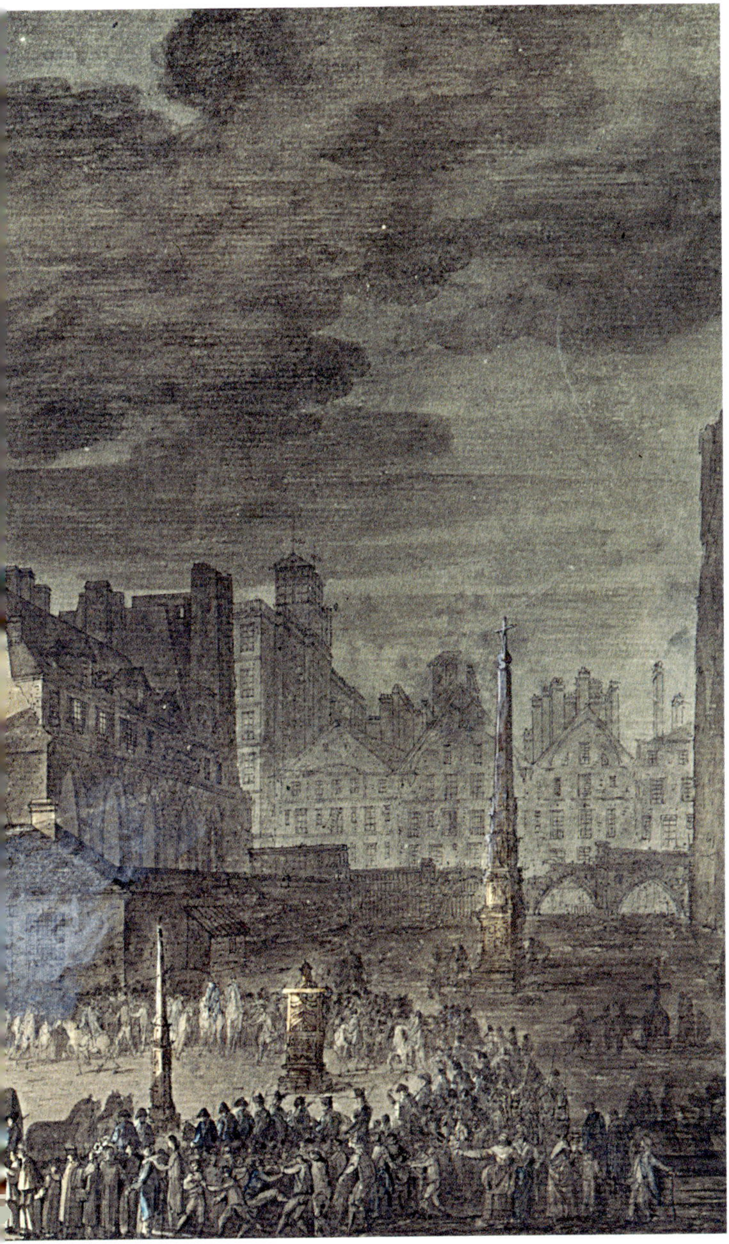

DESCRIPTION BY LOUIS-ÉTIENNE FRANÇOIS HÉRICART DE THURY

'The long procession of funerary carts and catafalques laden with bones slowly en route in the dusk to deposit these sad remains in the new Catacombs prepared outside the city walls, the sight of these vast subterranean vaults that seem to separate them from the land of the living, the contemplation of those present, the sombre clarity of the place, its profound silence, the horrible din of dry bones thrown and rolling, echoed by distant vaults, everything in these moments conjured the image of death.'

fig. 47
View of the Église des Innocents and presbytery before its 1787 demolition. Drawing by Jean-Nicolas Sobre (1750–1806), Musée Carnavalet, Paris.

An underground ossuary

Taking the Catacombs in Rome as his model, Jean-Charles-Pierre Lenoir, lieutenant-general of the city's police and provost and viscount of Paris, decided to create a new cemetery on the Tombe-Issoire plain to the south of Paris and a subterranean ossuary in the abandoned quarries beneath the site. The choice of this location was prompted by the large expanses of vacant land available there and access to the quarries. As the situation was urgent, work began in the 'lower cemetery'. The project for an open-air cemetery was forgotten during the Revolution.

fig. 48
Bones heaped at the bottom of an access shaft.

It was the General Inspector of Quarries, Guillaumot, who was charged with organising the site and identifying the subterranean galleries in which to deposit bones. He began by separating the ossuary space from the rest of the quarry by a boundary wall, consolidating it with masonry pillars.

The bones were tipped into the quarry via a service shaft on the Voie-Creuse, now Rue Dareau, on the site of the Maison de la Tombe-Issoire, recently acquired by the Inspectorate. A second access shaft and a staircase were created.

Visitors entered via the Barrière d'Enfer, then walked a long path through the quarries leading from the Médicis aqueduct. The new necropolis was inaugurated on 7 April 1786 and consecrated in the presence of priests from several parishes, representatives of the General Inspectorate of Quarries and a host of inquisitive bystanders. The ossuary became known as the 'Catacombs' after its Roman forebear.

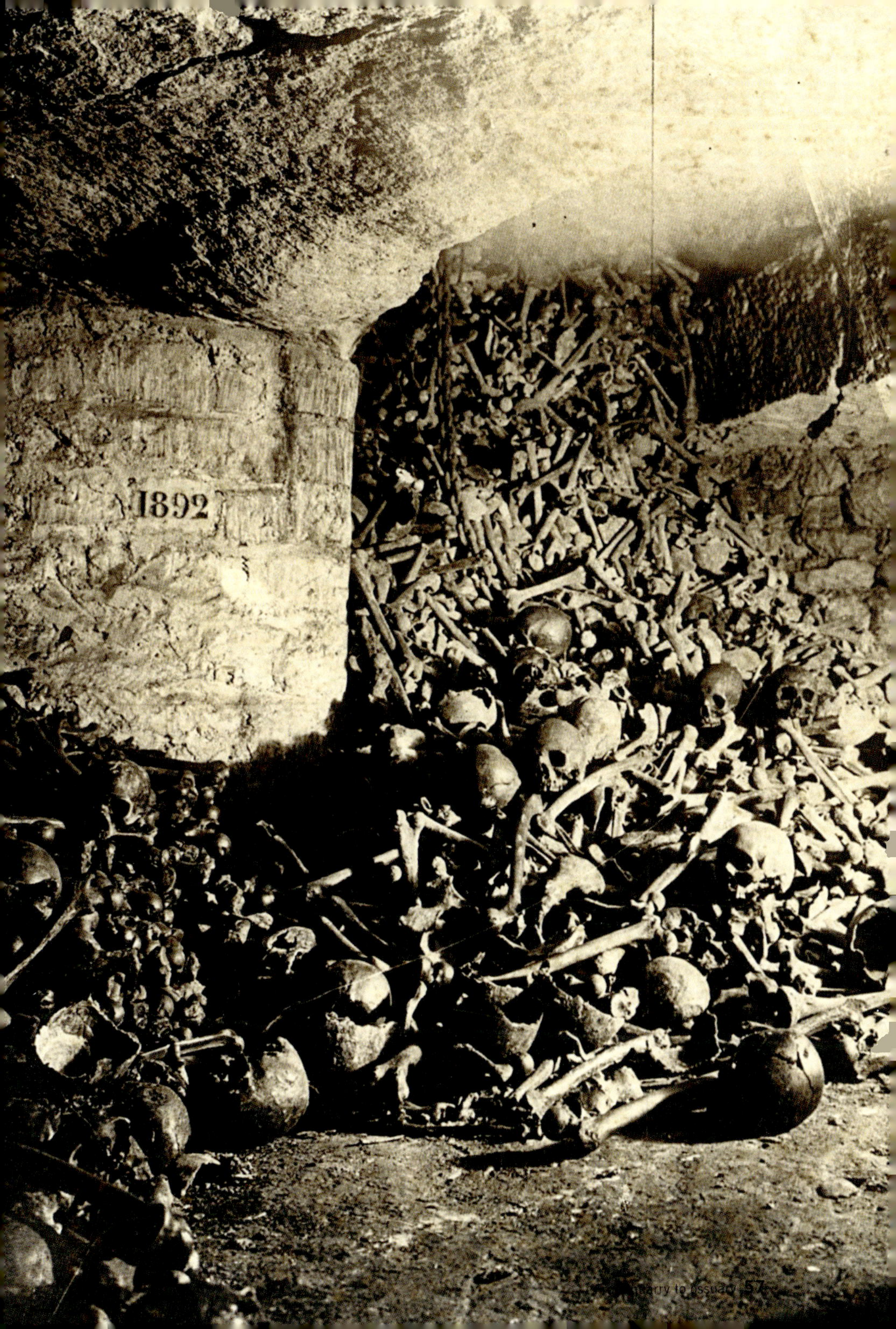
1892

Transfers of bones after 1786

Transfers of bones continued, encouraged by the success of the initial operation and the space still vacant. The Saint-Eustache and Saint-Étienne-des-Grès cemeteries, which were also declared infected, were emptied in 1787.

From 1788 the ossuary was used as a morgue and sepulchre for the Parisians who died during the Revolution: those who rioted outside the Hôtel de Brienne on 29 August 1788, the workers of the Réveillon manufactory in the Faubourg Saint-Antoine whose public protest ended in a massacre on 28 April 1789, and the hundreds who died during the fighting between insurgents and the Swiss Guards in the Tuileries on 10 August 1792. The corpses of many of the more than a thousand of inmates massacred in Paris's prisons between 2 and 6 September the same year were also taken to the Catacombs. The cemeteries of churches sold by the Nation as national property were evacuated: Saint-Landry and Saint-Julien-des-Ménétriers in 1792, Sainte-Croix-de-la-Bretonnerie in 1793, Saint-André-des-Arts in 1794, Saint-Esprit-en-Grève in 1803, Saint-Jean-en-Grève and the Blancs-Manteaux convent in 1804, and the Cauchin monastery in Saint-Honoré and the Petit-Saint-Antoine and Saint-Esprit in 1806. Transfers increased from the 1840s onwards as bones were unearthed during the urban redevelopment projects ordered by Louis-Philippe. Deposits continued intermittently until the 1960s as bones were sporadically unearthed by archaeological excavations.

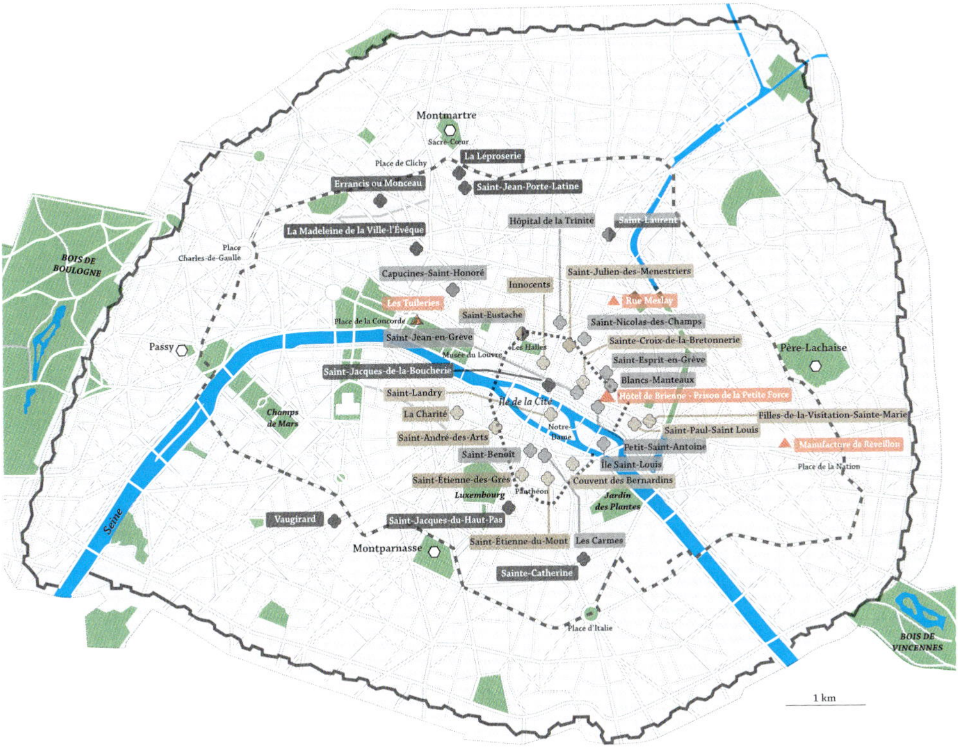

fig. 49
Map of Paris indicating the origins of its principal churches, whose cemeteries, mass graves and ossuaries were transferred to the Catacombs.

Transfer dates

- Between 1787 and 1800
- Between 1800 and 1814
- After 1817
- Victims of riots and massacres transfered in 1714

- Cemeteries created in the 18th century
- Boundary walls
- Thiers: 1840
- Farmers General
- Philippe Auguste

The improvements made by Louis-Étienne François Héricart de Thury

Nicolas Frochot (1761–1828), prefect of the Seine and Paris during the Consulate and the First Empire, embarked on a new programme of modernisation and sanitisation of the capital. Best known for the creation of the large Parisian cemeteries (Père-Lachaise, Montmartre, Montparnasse and Passy), then outside the city limits, Frochot also masterminded the present-day organisation and configuration of the Catacombs.

After Guillaumot died in 1807, he entrusted the redevelopment of the Catacombs to Héricart de Thury, appointed head of the General Inspectorate of Quarries in 1809, who began by consolidating the galleries beneath the Médicis aqueduct and in the Catacombs. He also organised the air circulation, reinforced the retaining pillars and moved the bones that had remained heaped at the bottom of the shafts into which they had been unloaded.

fig. 50
Sacellum crypt. The obelisks' altar is an 1810 copy of an Antique tomb.

fig. 51
Place du Memento, Simonet, Musée Carnavalet, Paris, 1812.

To give the ossuary an imposing appearance, he built monumental-looking columns, giving them bombastic names borrowed from Antiquity and literature such as the Memento Pillar, the Sarcophagus of the Lacrymatory (improperly called 'Gilbert's Tomb'), the Sacellum of the Obelisks and the Pillar of Clementine Nights.

The bones were arranged according to the medieval tradition and enhanced with new decorations left to the quarrymen's discretion. Their methods, a combination of masonry and the 'hagues et bourrages' technique, consisted in building a façade of long bones and skulls retaining the bones heaped behind.

The alternation of these walls of bones and monuments gave the Catacombs the dignified appearance of a mauso-

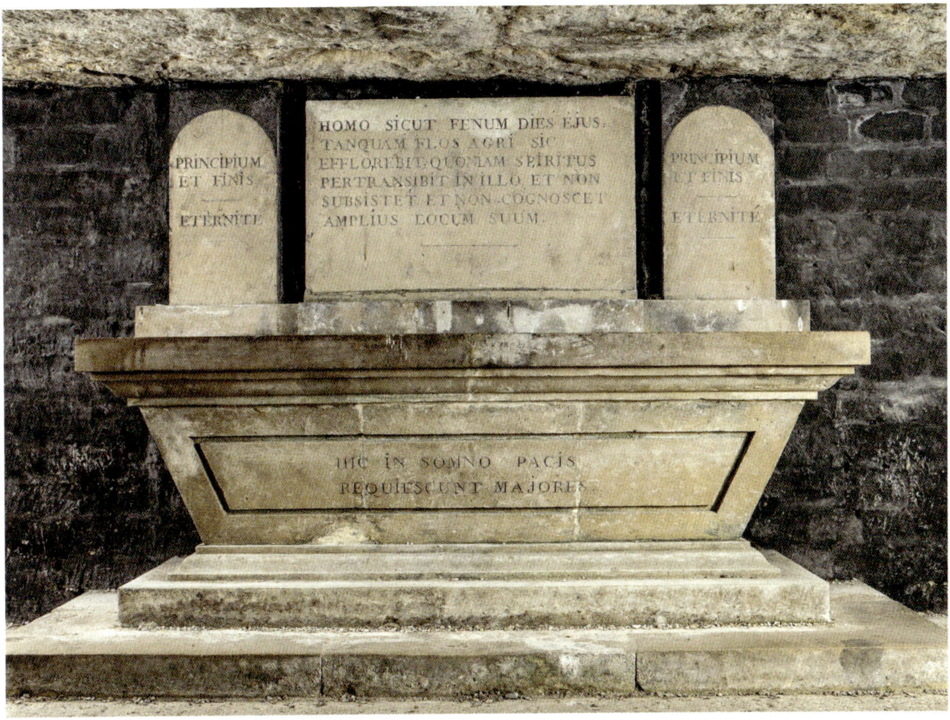
PRINCIPIUM
ET FINIS
ÉTERNITÉ
HOMO SICUT FENUM DIES EJUS
TANQUAM FLOS AGRI SIC
EFFLOREBIT QUONIAM SPIRITUS
PERTRANSIBIT IN ILLO ET NON
SUBSISTET ET NON COGNOSCET
AMPLIUS LOCUM SUUM.
PRINCIPIUM
ET FINIS
ÉTERNITÉ
HIC IN SOMNO PACIS
REQUIESCUNT MAJORES

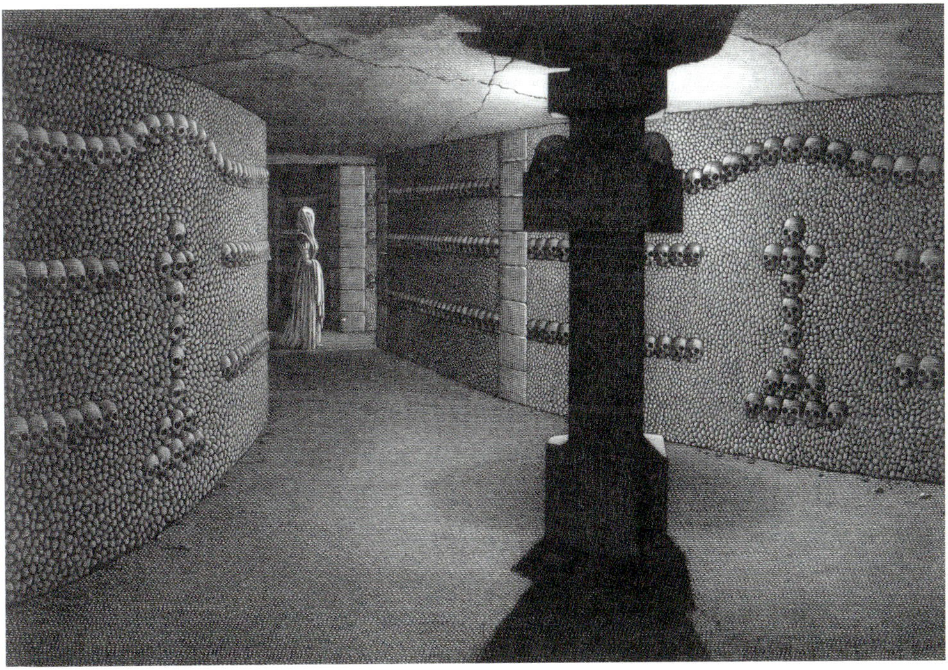

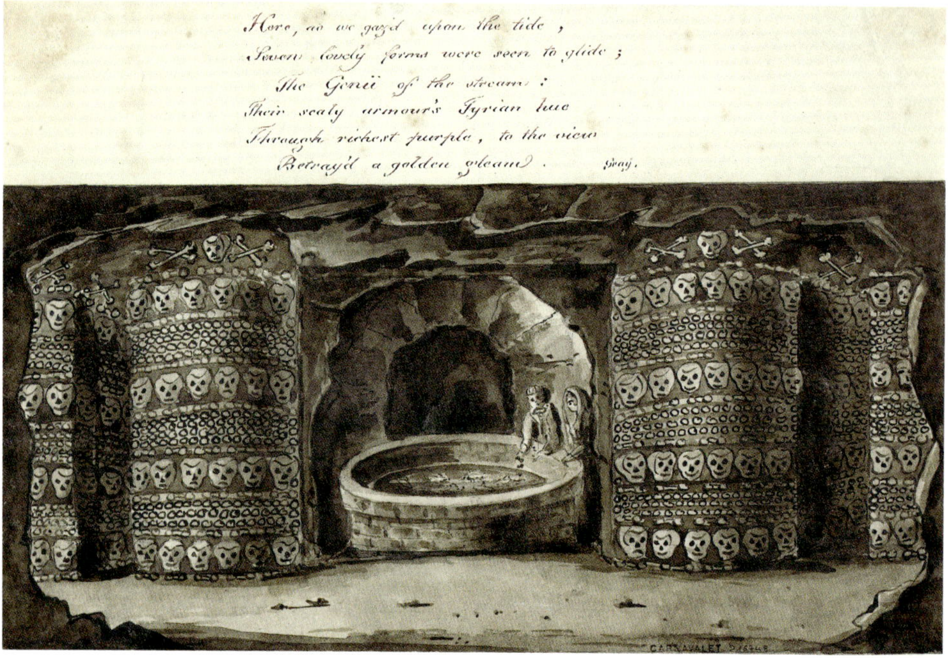
Here, as we gaz'd upon the tide,
Seven lovely forms were seen to glide;
The Genii of the stream:
Their scaly armour's Tyrian hue
Through richest purple, to the view
Betray'd a golden gleam. Gray.

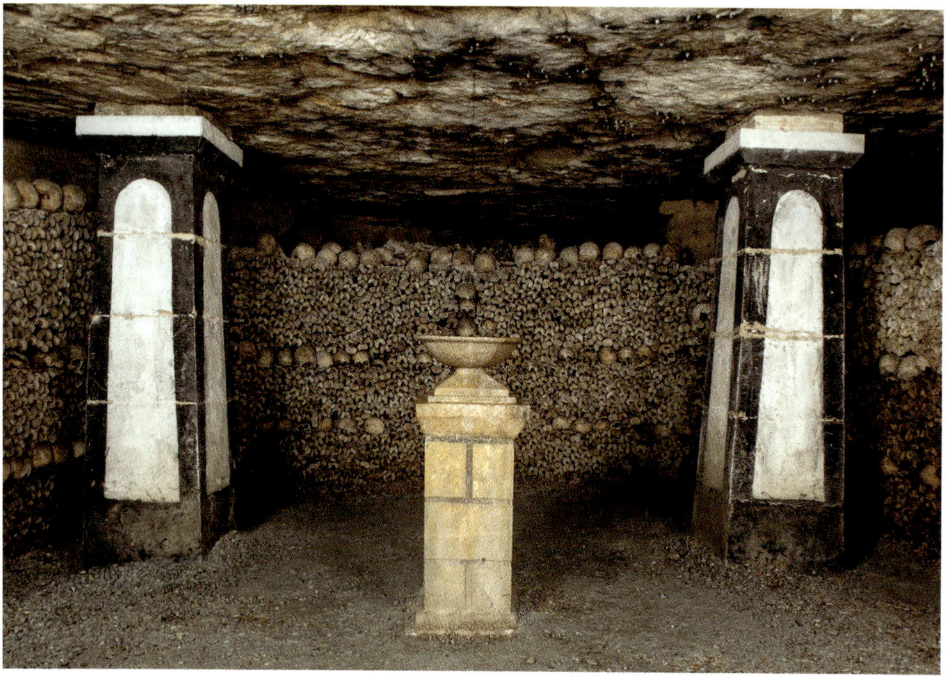

fig. 52
View of the Fountain of Forgetting, also called 'the Samaritan Woman'. Drawing by James Forbes (1749–1861), lead and India ink, Musée Carnavalet, Paris.

leum and filled visitors with a powerful mixture of respect, contemplation and dread.

The Catacombs, opened to the public on 1 July 1809, was one of the very first Parisian museums, proposing to its visitors not collections of fine art but a tour of the ossuary conceived as an underground landscaped park.

Practical monuments

The monuments in the Catacombs serve a structural purpose and conceal reinforcement masonry, and the same is true of two other additions, the Fountain of the Samaritan Woman and the Sepulchral Lamp, whose prime purpose is eclipsed by their decorative aspect.

fig. 53
The Sepulchral Lamp

Quarrymen hollowed out a reservoir to collect water from an underground spring to mix the mortar for their masonry reinforcements. The original ramp became a staircase, and a circular alternation of pillars and 'hagues' of bones was created around the reservoir. To accentuate its solemnity, the place was baptised the 'Fountain of Lethe', 'of oblivion' or 'of the Samaritan Woman'. This reservoir was also used for attempts to acclimatise goldfish to a subterranean environment and study their evolution and reproduction.

The Sepulchral Lamp, the first monument built in the visitors' galleries, consists of a bowl on a pedestal, whose purpose was to maintain a fire burning underground so creating air currents and an artificial ventilation system.

The ossuary's signage and installation

As the bones were being transferred in 1786, despite the stipulation that the cemetery they came from be respected and indicated, part of the remains were dispersed, probably because operations were supervised only on the surface. Intent on restoring some order to this chaotic situation, Héricart de Thury installed signs and engraved steles indicating the bones' origins and the date of their transfer to the Catacombs.

fig. 54
Plaque commemorating the Cimetière de Saint-Eustache, 1787.

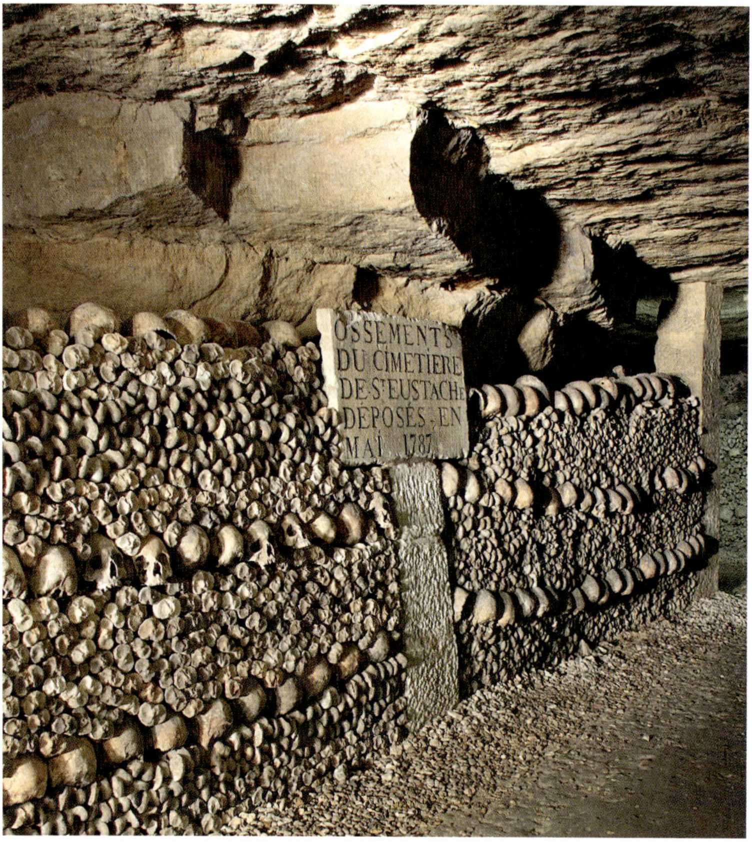

fig. 55
Plaque commemorating the Cimetière des Innocents, 1787.

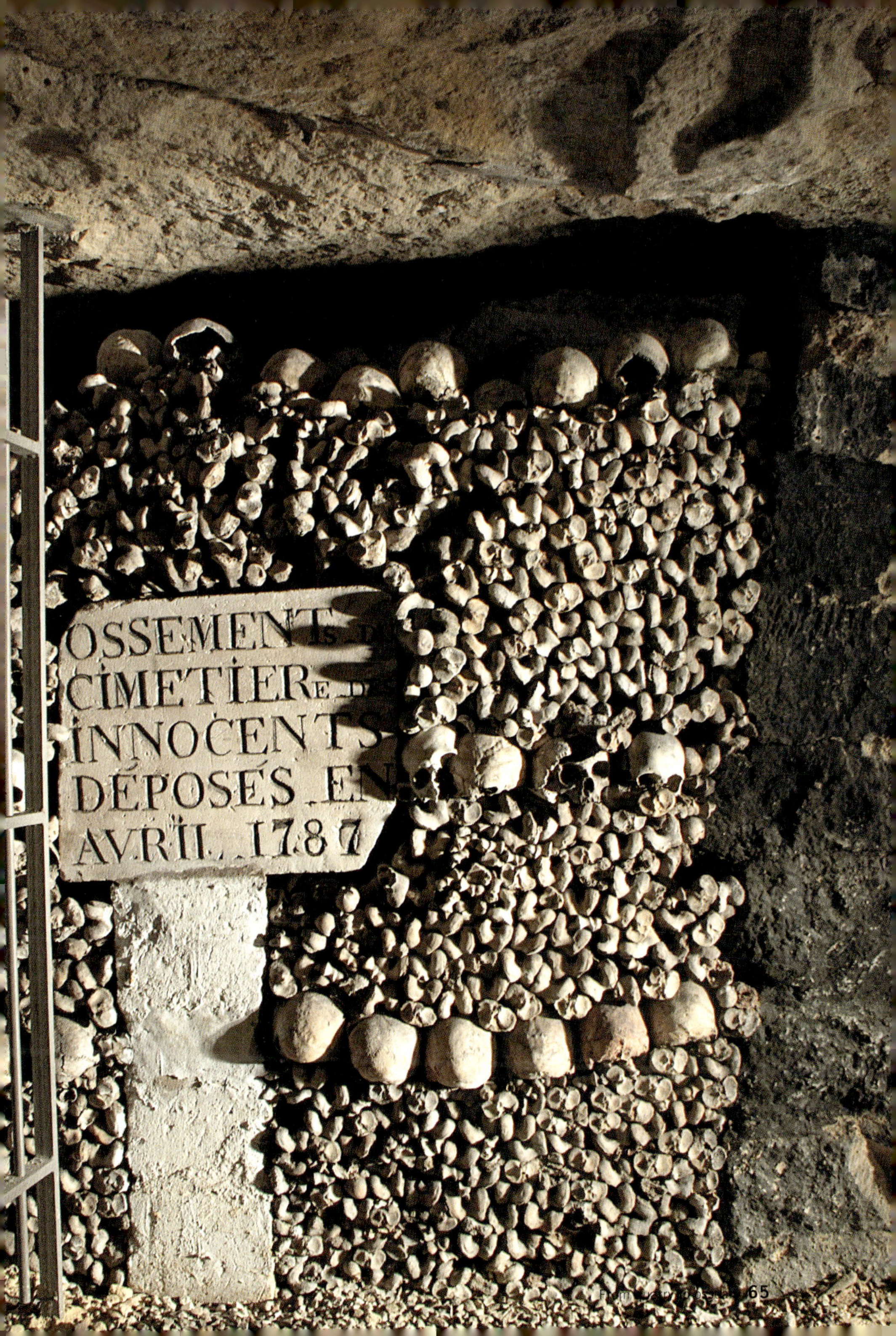
OSSEMENTS D
CIMETIERE D
INNOCENTS
DÉPOSÉS EN
AVRIL 1787

Macabre literary inscriptions

The Catacombs are full of stones engraved with literary inscriptions, a veritable anthology of macabre and funerary prose and poetry reflecting the tastes and influences of the time: the English Gothic novel, the Romantic movement in art and literature and the renewed interest in Greco-Roman Antiquity. They also reflect the cultivated personality of Héricart de Thury, who chose religious and profane texts, often emphatic and of varying quality, whose central theme is the inexorability of death.

fig. 56
Pillar with engraved inscription.

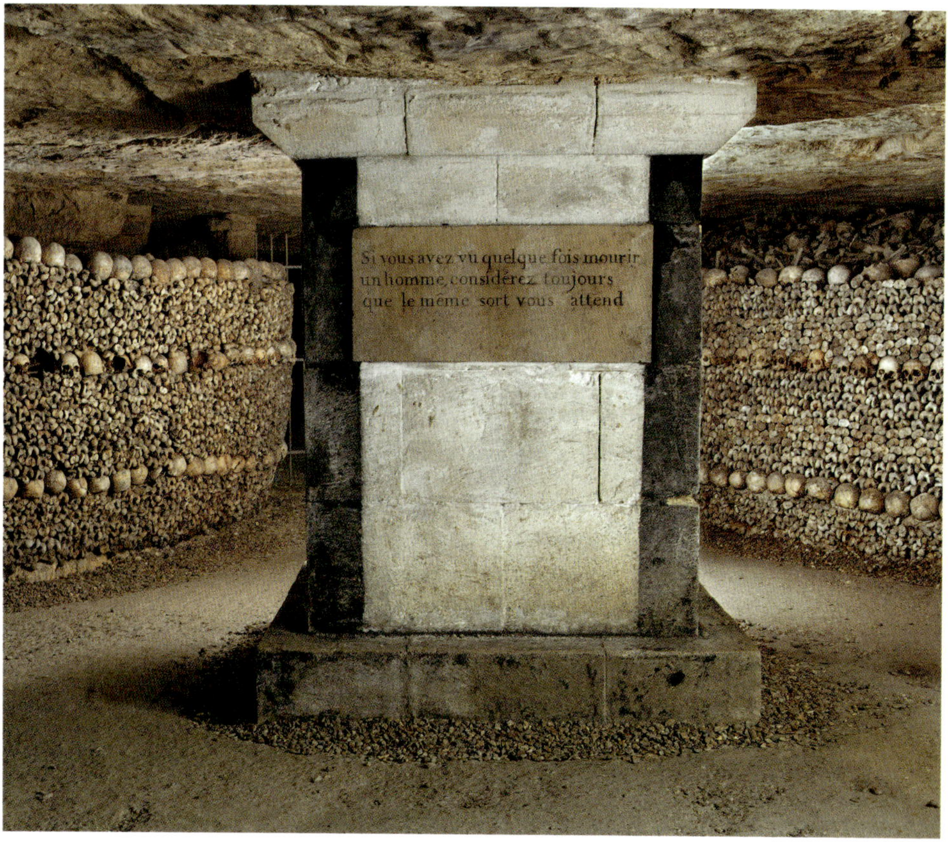

A place of scientific research and experimentation

In 1809 the prefect Frochot, aware of the scientific interest of the Catacombs, authorised their access to scientists and scholars. Less than a century later, two researchers from the National Museum of Natural History used the galleries to carry out research into life in subterranean environments. The botanist Jacques Maheu studied flora capable of growing without light, and the speleologist and naturalist Armand Viré revealed the existence of cave-dwelling crustaceans. In 1897, he studied their development in a labora-

fig. 57
The Fountain of the Samaritan Woman with four visitors: Jacques Maheu, Armand Viré, Prince Bibesco and A. Brongniard. Early 20th century. Viré Collection.

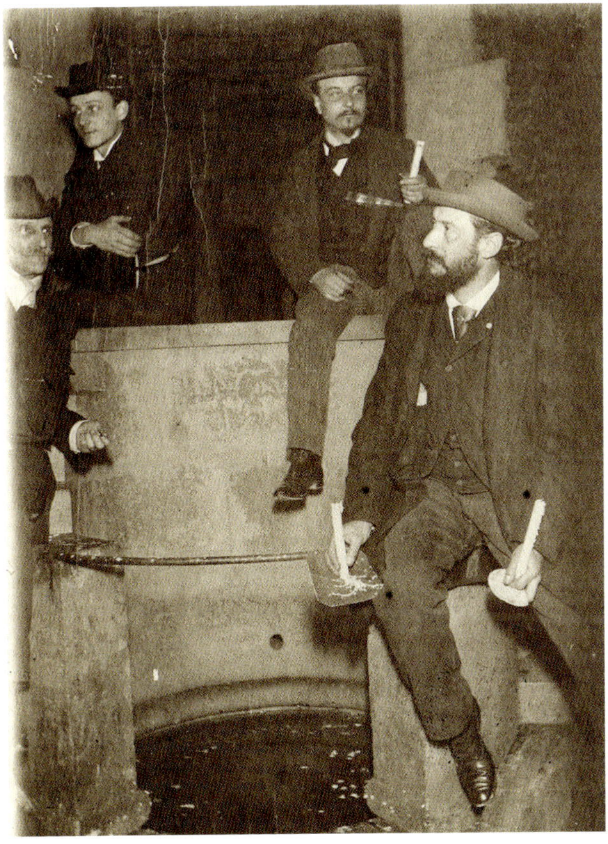

tory in a gallery in the disused quarry beneath the Museum of Natural History in the Jardin des Plantes.

A mineralogy display in the tradition of Renaissance cabinets of curiosities and in the scientific spirit of the 19th century was created for the general public. On the second floor of the Port-Mahon gallery but no longer in existence, this pioneering pedagogical presentation explained the quarry's geological stratigraphy, showing the successive layers of limestone extracted.

Nadar and the first photographs taken in artificial light

In 1861, Félix Tournachon, known as Nadar, obtained permission from Inspector Fourcy to work in the ossuary. He had just taken the first aerial photographs of Paris from an aerostat, and now spent three months photographing the Catacombs and the city's sewers, taking the first photographs with artificial light. To do so, he devised a new electric lighting technique using enormous accumulators, Bunsen batteries and reflectors. As the exposure time of these photographs was very long (up to eighteen minutes), he dressed mannequins as quarrymen and arranged them in working poses. He recounts these 'black rendezvous with the immense void' in his memoirs.

fig. 58
Photograph by Nadar, 1861.

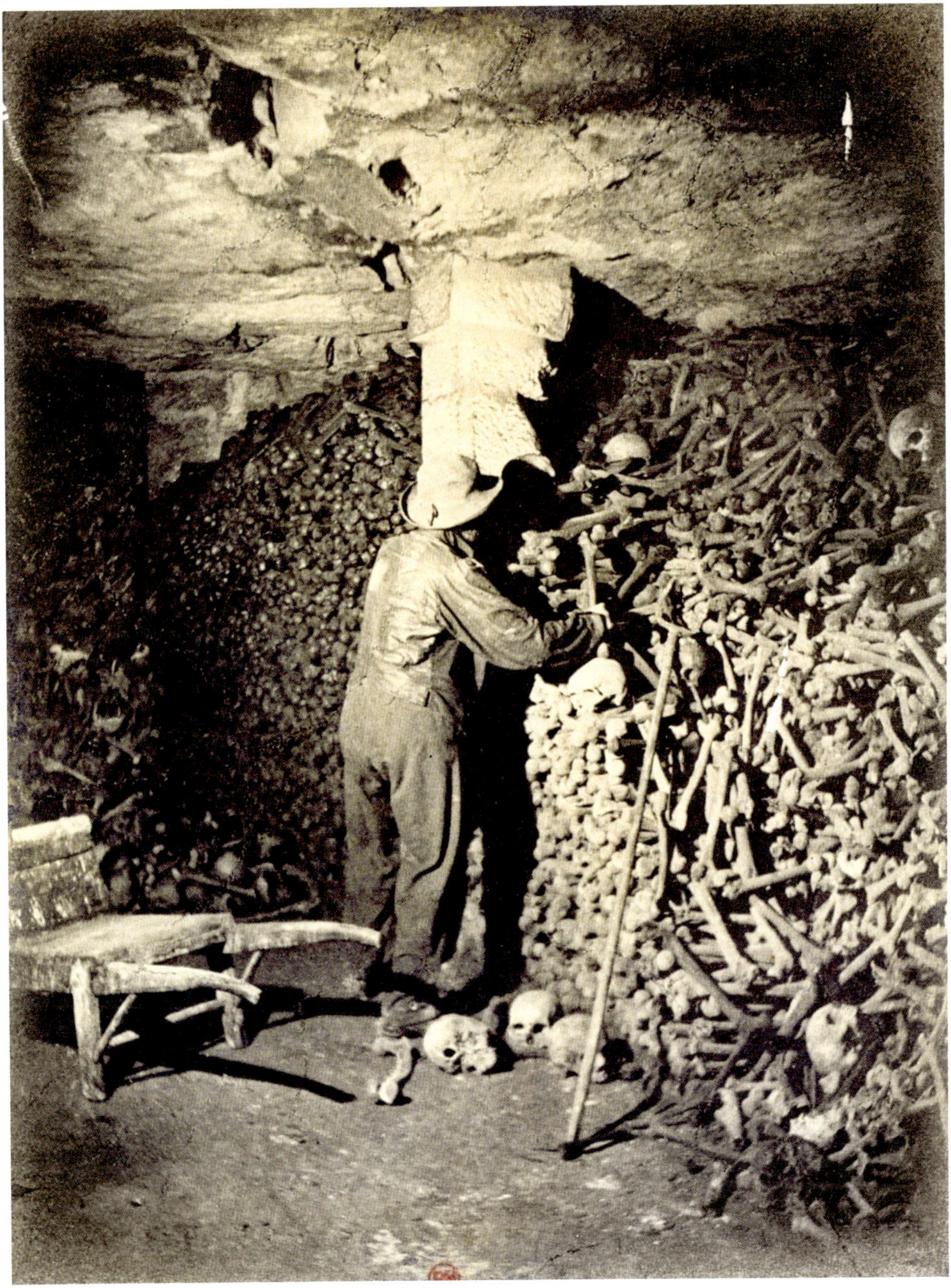

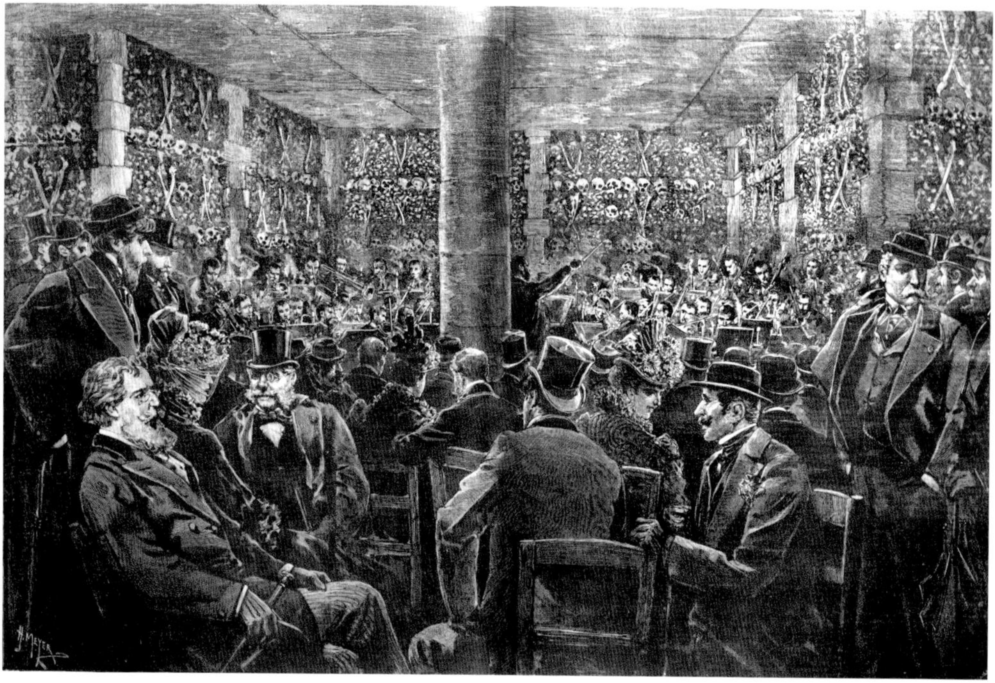

A fashionable rendezvous for people in search of thrills

On 2 April 1897, a concert was organised in a part of the ossuary called the 'Crypt of Passion' or 'Rotunda of the Tibias'. According to *Le Figaro,* around a hundred people attended the performance. The pieces the orchestra played included Chopin's *Funeral March* and Camille Saint-Saëns's *Danse macabre*. The latter work was considered the most impressive piece in this macabre programme. In this symphonic poem, composed in 1874 and based on a text by Henri Cazalis, every instrument plays a role, with the xylophone imitating the rattle of bones.

fig. 59
Concert performed in the Paris Catacombs. Engraving by Navellier after a drawing by Henri Meyer. *Le Journal illustré*, 18 April 1897.

In Gaston Leroux's 1903 novel *La Double Vie de Théophraste Longuet* (published in English as *The Double Life*), its heroes, Mifroid and Longuet, lost in the quarry galleries, find their way thanks to the candles lighting the famous concert. At the time, the Catacombs were open once a month, and only to visitors with a special pass.

'We have before us fifty musicians from the Opéra, Lamoureux and Colonne orchestras, who have descended into the kingdom of the dead to serenade the departed. And beneath the vaults of the Catacombs, among the avenues and crossroads lined with tragic walls of skulls, tibias and femurs, the plea of Chopin's *Funeral March* is heard by an audience of aesthetes and artists' tiny famished stomachs...' (Chapter 38, 'Un joyeux ossuaire')

The hero deplores the invasion of this subterranean world by Parisians in search of thrills, who come to disturb the integrity of the quarries and the ossuary with 'midnights parties given by those who are civilised above ground', 'all the artistic-mystic-macabre scenes in which life is ridiculed and death is laughed at', 'the nocturnal rape of the immense pit by the alcoholic laughter of local tarts'.

An imaginary world

In the second half of the 19th century, a number of novelists exploited the popular fascination for subterranean Paris in a new genre of fantastic and ghoulish literature. Paris's cavernous 'basement' became a refuge for a supernatural, evil population and for bandits of all kinds.

This nefarious reputation was based on historical fact. In the 16th and 17th centuries, the underground network of quarries became a lair for smugglers, who could fraudulently bring goods into Paris via their galleries without paying the excise duty levied at the city's gates.

An initial order voted by Paris's parliament in 1548 mentions the banditry that had developed in the quarries along the Route d'Orléans, now Avenue Général-Leclerc (14th arrondissement). The inhabitants of the Faubourg Saint-Jacques were responsible for their surveillance. Fifteen years later, a second order obliged quarrymen to close the entrances to the quarries during the night to prevent bandits from entering.

Until the Revolution little was known about the nocturnal life in Paris's underground quarries, which was rendered even more mysterious by legends intended to deter visitors, such as that of the wandering ghost called 'the Green Man'.

THE LEGEND OF THE VAUVERT DEVIL

In the 12th century, bandits took over the quarries beneath the present-day Luxembourg Gardens, entering them via the ruins of the Hôtel de Val-Vert, built by the son of Hugues Capet. They terrorised the local population, who regarded the noises and lights of their nocturnal activities as manifestations of the Devil, and the Val-Vert quarries became the home of the mythical 'Diable Vauvert'.

THE TRAGEDY OF PHILIBERT ASPAIRT

In the Catacombs and quarries, one could easily get buried by subsidences and above all get lost. The true or fictional story of Philibert Aspairt illustrates the fear of remaining trapped in this subterranean labyrinth. Aspairt, a porter in the Val-de-Grâce Convent, had the idea of passing through the underground quarries to the Chartreux Convent to rob its cellar of its famous liqueur. He lost his way, and his corpse, identifiable by his bunch of keys, was discovered by quarrymen eleven years later, in 1804.

The Catacombs, a source of literary inspiration

In 1832, Élie Berthet set the plot of one of his popular novels in the Catacombs. *Les Catacombes de Paris* was so successful that the story was still serialised in *Le Journal du*

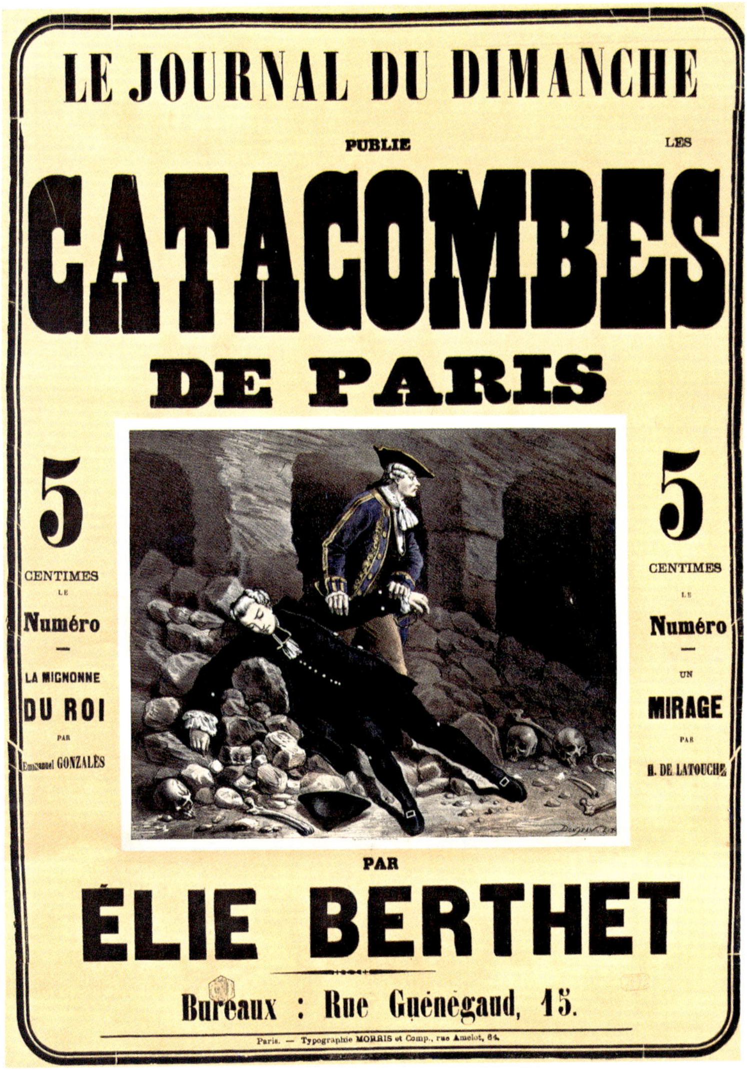

fig. 60
Poster for the publication of *Catacombes de Paris* by Élie Berthet in *Le Journal du dimanche*, Gustave Donjean, 1865.

dimanche thirty years later. Its hero, Philippe de Lussan, frees his beloved Thérèse, held captive by the quarryman Médard. The Catacombs are again the setting for Joseph Méry's novel *Salons et souterrains de Paris*: 'To the right and left, in beautiful symmetrical order, were aligned layers of human bones whose blackish tint announced their age. This gloomy decoration could still be seen in the dim glow of the lamp, at infernal crossroads beneath the vaults of galleries which appeared to prolong this double basement of death into infinity (vol. 1, p. 1, Paris, 1852).

In *Salvator* (1855–1859), Alexandre Dumas set Police Superintendent Jackal's pursuit of the Carbonari (a secret revolutionary society) in the quarries, and in *Les Misérables* Victor Hugo describes a group of bandits that ran rampant in Paris and established their headquarters in the underground quarries: 'The moment has come to glimpse other, hideous depths'. 'A quartet of bandits, Claquesous, Gueulemer, Babet and Montparnasse, governed the lowest depths of Paris from 1830 to 1835.' 'These beings, who were very cautious about showing their faces, were not the sort of people one normally sees on the streets. By day, wearied by their wild nights, they went to sleep sometimes in the lime kilns, sometimes in the abandoned quarries of Montmartre or Montrouge and sometimes in the sewers. They went to ground.' (Victor Hugo, *Les Misérables*, vol. 3, *Marius*, 1862, book 7, chapters 2, 3 and 4)

In 19th-century literature, Paris's underground world was a dark, forbidden world of violence and debauchery, but also of exploration and adventure. This is still true in 21st-century comic books, graphic novels by French-speaking authors and video games.

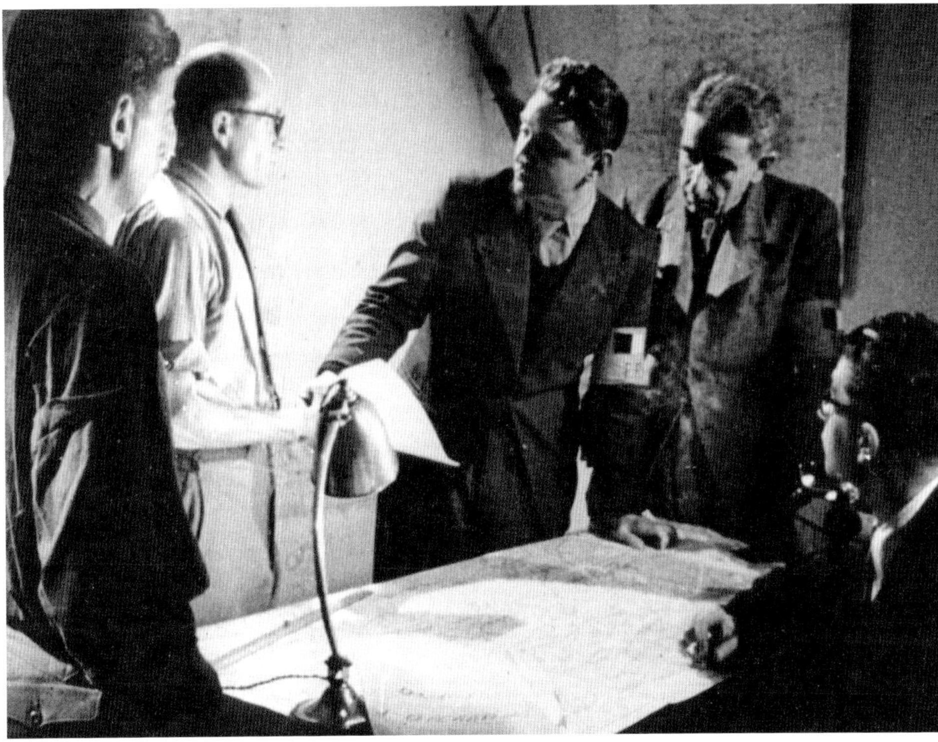

fig. 61
Henri Rol-Tanguy at his command post, August 1944.

THE CATACOMBS AT THE HEART OF THE LIBERATION OF PARIS

The Catacombs played their final role in the liberation of the capital in August 1944. From 1 June, Henri Rol-Tanguy, a resistance fighter in the Francs-Tireurs et Partisans (FTP), became regional commander of the headquarters of the Forces Françaises de l'Intérieur (FFI). He set up his command post beneath Place Denfert-Rochereau, at a depth of 26 metres, in a shelter linked by underground galleries to the terminus of the Seaux railway line and to the quarries and Catacombs. He could also telephone all the service posts of Paris's water and sewage system.

The Catacombs today: a complex heritage to manage

In the last quarter of the 20th century illicit frequentation of the underground quarries increased and the Catacombs, visits to which, until then, had been marginal and respectful of these historic places, and resulted in acts of vandalism jeopardising their conservation: graffiti, accumulations of litter and rubbish and destructions of the quarries' ancient consolidations. The deterioration of the quarries and the Catacombs caused by these clandestine intrusions and the particularly humid climatic conditions jeopardising the preservation of the ossuaries now represent a dual challenge. Maintained since they were opened by the General Inspectorate of Quarries, since 2002 the Catacombs have been managed by the Musée Carnavalet, which is pursuing the site's protection and improvement. Recent preventive conservation studies have established procedures for the upkeep of the walls of bones, and analyses of the ambient atmosphere have enabled considerable improvements to climatic conditions underground.

fig. 62
Detail of the ossuary decoration.

The restoration of the ossuary is now underway, respecting the original decorations and paying particular attention to the management of human remains. Enhancing awareness of the geological and archaeological heritage of the quarries and the historical legacy of the ossuary are the keystones of this museum project.

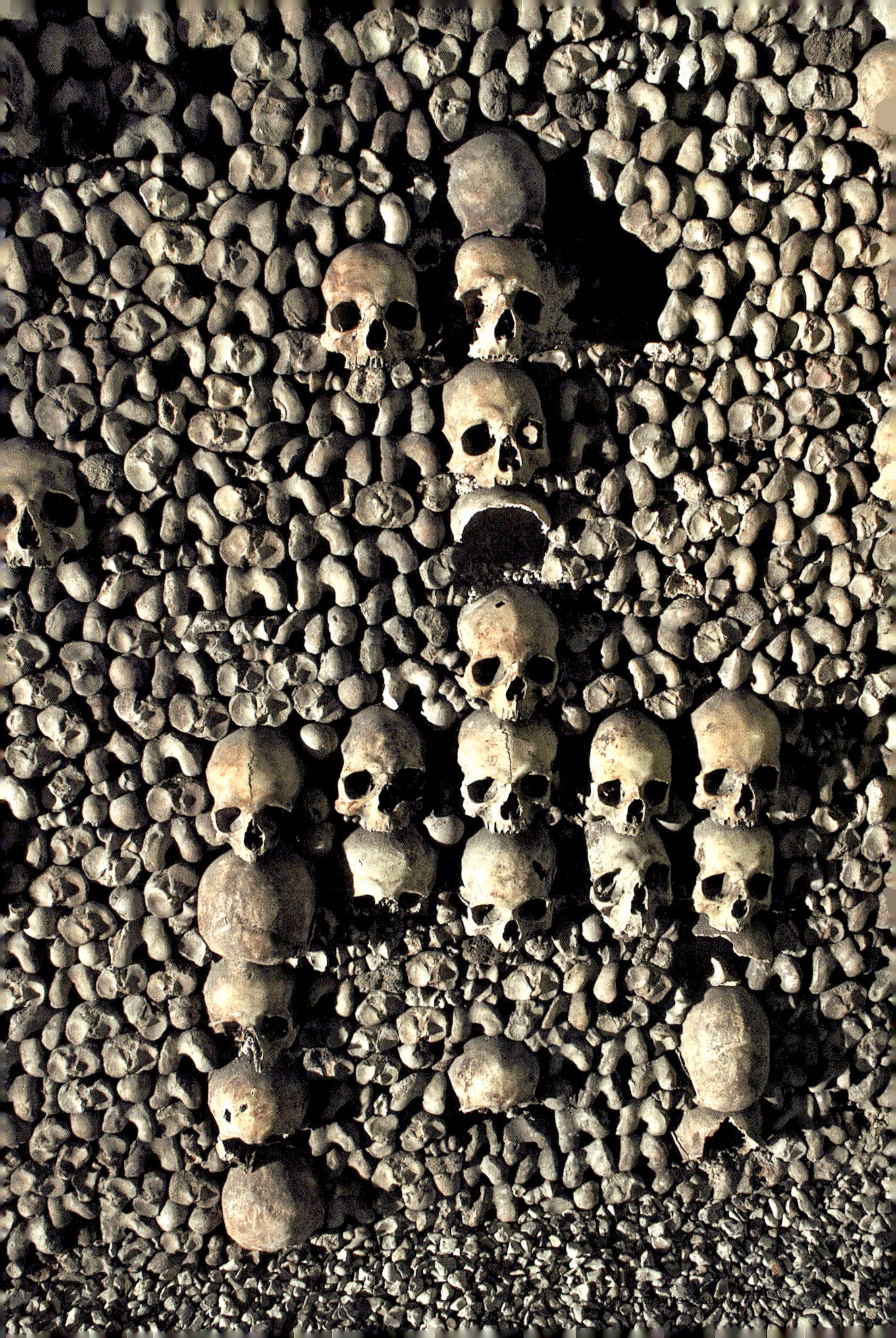

List of illustrations

Bibliography

Louis-Étienne François Héricart de Thury, *Description des Catacombes de Paris* (Paris: Bossange et Masson, 1815; Paris: Comité des travaux historiques et scientifiques, 1999).

Émile Gérards, *Paris souterrain* (Garnier Frères: 1908) (Torcy: DMI Édition, 1991).

René Suttel, *Catacombes et carrières de Paris* (Châtillon: Éditions du Treuil, 1993).

Ania Guini-Skliar, Marc Viré, Jacqueline Lorenz, Jean-Pierre Gély and Annie Blanc, *Les Souterrains de Paris. Les anciennes carrières souterraines* (Cambray: Nord Patrimoine, 2000).

Delphine Cerf and David Babinet, *Les Catacombes de Paris* (Meudon: Moulenq, 1994).

Ania Guini-Skliar, "La Pierre à bâtir dans l'architecture parisienne (XVIe-XVIIIe siècle)", PhD thesis, Université François-Rabelais de Tours, 1998.

Paris Musées
Director
Delphine Lévy
Exhibitions and publications
Director
Olivier Donat
Deputy director
Julie Bertrand
Head of the Publishing Department
Isabelle Jendron

The Catacombs of Paris
Director
Valérie Guillaume

The authors would like to sincerely thank the following for their advice and aid:
Florence Cavaillé and Anne-Marie Prunier Leparmentier (General Inspectorate of Quarries), Jacqueline Lorenz and Blaise Souffaché (Université Paris-VI), Stéphane Volland and the staff of the Catacombs, Jean-Marie Bruson, Valérie Guillaume, Gérard Leyris, Michèle Margueron, Pauline Noirot, Thierry Sarmant (musée Carnavalet), Christinne Levisse-Touzé, director of the musée du Général-Leclerc-de-Hautecloque et de la Libération, Marc Le Mené, Rose-Marie Mousseaux.

Graphic design
Agnès Rousseaux
Editorial coordination
Maryse Vaissière
Translation from French to English
David Wharry
Copyediting
Bronwyn Mahoney
Photographic rights
Laurence Goupille
Aurélie Fouré
assisted by Sophie Bodénan
Production
Mara Mariano
Saint-Véron Pompée
Colour separation
Planète Couleurs, Paris
Paper
Gardamatt Ultra, 130 g

27, rue des Petites-Écuries
75010 Paris

Diffusion Flammarion
Distribution UD-Union
Distribution
ISBN 978-2-7596-0266-7
ISSN 1958-0800
Legal deposit: June 2014
Printed by D'Auria Printing (Italy), January 2018

The cover of this book is printed with a phosphorescent varnish